# THE
# TRAINER
# TOOLKIT

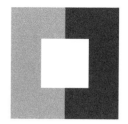

# THE TRAINER TOOLKIT

### ALISON BORTHWICK • PAUL ELLIS • MARK WINTERBOTTOM

A GUIDE TO DELIVERING TRAINING IN SCHOOLS

CORWIN

A SAGE company
2455 Teller Road
Thousand Oaks, California 91320
(0800)233-9936
www.corwin.com

SAGE Publications Ltd
1 Oliver's Yard
55 City Road
London EC1Y 1SP

SAGE Publications India Pvt Ltd
B 1/I 1 Mohan Cooperative Industrial Area
Mathura Road
New Delhi 110 044

SAGE Publications Asia-Pacific Pte Ltd
3 Church Street
#10-04 Samsung Hub
Singapore 049483

First published in 2020

Editor: Amy Thornton
Senior project editor: Chris Marke
Project management: Deer Park Productions, Tavistock, Devon
Marketing manager: Dilhara Attygalle
Cover design: Wendy Scott
Typeset by: C&M Digitals (P) Ltd, Chennai, India
Printed in the UK

**Library of Congress Control Number: 2019954064**

**British Library Cataloguing in Publication data**

A catalogue record for this book is available from the British Library

ISBN 978-1-5264-9372-9
ISBN 978-1-5264-9371-2 (pbk)

# CONTENTS

# LIST OF FIGURES AND TABLES

## FIGURES

## TABLES

# ABOUT THE AUTHORS

 **Alison Borthwick** is an international education adviser. She has worked with many different organisations, universities and professional associations both in the UK and abroad. Her portfolio is underpinned by her experience as a teacher, leader, trainer and researcher. An experienced education consultant, Alison has written numerous books and papers for teachers.

 **Paul Ellis** began teaching in schools and universities in the 1990s and has held senior positions in two of the main international education providers since 2006. Within his current role, he is in charge of the worldwide recruitment and development of teacher-trainers. He has worked with teachers and school leaders on all continents to advise and support them in their professional learning. He has written or edited more than a dozen education books.

 **Mark Winterbottom** is a Senior Lecturer in Education at the Faculty of Education, University of Cambridge. He has been extensively involved in teacher professional development and curriculum development in the UK and abroad. During his 20 years in education, he has authored a number of school textbooks and books for teachers.

We would like to thank our families.

We would also like to dedicate this book to the teachers we have trained, for all the enjoyment we have shared and for all we have learnt from you.

# INTRODUCTION

## KEYWORDS IN THIS CHAPTER

- what
- why
- who
- when
- how
- trainer
- teacher
- handbook
- authors

- experience
- reader
- tools
- ideas
- advice
- skills
- questions
- expectations

## WHAT?

Welcome to *The Trainer Toolkit.*

We have written this book to help you train teachers and other education professionals. We are going to assume you that you have experience of working in or with schools. We are also presuming that you have expertise to pass on to other people. Perhaps you have already facilitated sessions for teaching colleagues and are looking for ways to get better at it? Perhaps you are about to train teachers for the very first time?

This is a handbook for anyone working in *continuing* professional development. It is for you, regardless of the phase, age, stage or subject in which you specialise. It is not specific to a certain syllabus, programme or exam board. Our aim is simply to give you the tools to be a fantastic trainer. We will talk you through what this means in detail, and we will also help you think about how to measure and evaluate your impact as a trainer.

# WHY?

The focus of this book is learning and teaching in schools, wherever you are in the world. We know from all the countries we have visited that teachers want and need professional development. Sometimes this is provided by external bodies, such as the state or the organisation that sets the exams for which your students are studying. Increasingly, though, teachers are getting professional development 'in-house' from their colleagues.

Training adults is not the same as teaching children. Although there is overlap (you might be surprised at the recalcitrant or unprofessional behaviour of some of your colleagues), we will tell you about some important considerations when working with adults. Don't assume because you are a trained teacher and may have been teaching for years that you will naturally be or feel like an expert when you stand up in front of your peers.

We are going to explore *why* and *how* teachers and education professionals learn, and what they expect from training. We will look together at the delivery of training, from the basics to the many useful, often quite subtle ideas we have developed or picked up over the years. Based on our work collectively and globally in over 50 countries, we will guide you through a series of recognised standards for being a trainer, sharing plenty of ideas that are easy to put into practice.

# WHO?

First and foremost, we have an image of you, the reader, as someone who has an active interest in the professional development of others. You will have reflected on what this means, or you will at least have given it some thought.

You might be a school leader, a middle or senior manager, or anyone, regardless of rank, who is required to facilitate or coordinate training and professional development for colleagues in your school or school group.

You might alternatively be an experienced trainer or someone who aspires to be one. You might be employed, full- or part-time, by an organisation or business specialising in education, or you might be pursuing a career independently as a freelance consultant trainer.

We can't claim to know every culture, but it is our intention to take into consideration how expectations and attitudes may vary, depending on where you are working. We will share with you our experiences of what works – and what might not – worldwide. The audience for this book is, therefore, somewhat varied, and you will need to explore your own context to decide whether some of the ideas will work. We hope, though, that there is a lot for everyone!

And you might be asking who *we* are? Well, above all we are teachers who have a dedicated interest in developing both children and adults. We have taught students from pre-school level to PhD, and, between us, we have trained and observed thousands of

teachers and teacher-trainers. Our subjects aren't important here, but, just so that you know, we have specialised in teaching languages, mathematics, sciences, humanities and the arts.

Our careers have taken us far beyond the classroom where we took our initial steps. We have been fortunate enough to be invited to travel and work with teachers in a wide range of countries in most corners of the globe. We have worked for schools, school groups, universities, exam boards and governments. It is our goal, wherever we go, both to teach and to learn. We decided to write this book, based on our experiences, to help you do the same.

## WHEN?

We won't be offended if this book sits on your shelf or in the professional development library of your school and is only picked up from time to time. We would like to think, though, that you will find multiple opportunities for reading or browsing it, or for recommending it to other people.

You might be planning a programme of professional development for teachers. You might have suddenly been asked to run a workshop next week, or maybe even tomorrow! You might have picked up this book to give you a refresher, or to help you reflect on what you do well.

It is a book to be read before, while and after you train teachers.

# HOW?

We have designed *The Trainer Toolkit* so that it has four distinct parts:

A.  Setting the scene
B.  Getting ready to train
C.  Training activities
D.  Evaluating and reflecting on your training and developing yourself as a trainer

In **Part A: Setting the scene**, we are going to ask you first to reflect on your *own* experiences of professional development. What was *good?* What could have been *better?*

We will next look at your *audience*. What might be their expectations of your training? How can you manage these expectations? What 'baggage' might they bring? What are the indicators, and how might you handle the baggage? What is it like working with people from different cultures? How should you prepare for the place where you will be training?

This brings us to the all-important question of how to work with *adults*. We will consider how to motivate adult learners, exploring some of the theories of andragogy (adult learning), as compared to pedagogy (children's learning). How can we facilitate training sessions in which we can encourage adults to be active rather than passive learners? And how do we help them know what to take away?

We then explore models for *disseminating* learning. In this we are talking above all about in-school training, where one teacher or another member of staff is asked to educate their colleagues. Essentially, we will look at how to empower you to train your peers. And lastly in this chapter, we will encourage you to think about the impact of your training, and how to ensure the outcomes are disseminated.

In **Part B: Getting ready to train**, we will look first at how you should *plan* your training sessions. We will start by exploring the purpose of a training session, how to set objectives, and what strategies and tactics to use.

We will begin to look in turn at how to create the conditions for success in training. What *rules* should you set? How can you break the ice? What *equipment* will you need? How much can you do in the *time* that you have? Where and when should you actively involve the audience? How will you scaffold their learning? How will you encourage them to share their experiences and expertise? How will you summarise what they should have learnt? How will they know?

Designing and understanding the purpose of the *materials* you use can be key to the success and lasting impact of your training. You might be asked to use materials designed by others: why might this be the case and what does it mean for your training? Or you might be free to design your own materials: how do you begin to do this, and what does it involve? We will also advise you on how to organise and present your materials.

The next focus is your training *environment*. Sometimes you have little choice about where you will be working, but you can still make a good initial impression. We will think about how to configure the room, how to maximise the space and even how to 'use' your audience! We will also say a few words about technology and other features of your training room.

And we close this part of the book by taking a close look at *presentation* skills. This starts with your own personal presentation: how should you look, how should you express yourself, how should you moderate your body language? We will help you think as well about verbal and written language, especially – but not only – for participants in your training whose first language differs from that of the training session. How can you be inclusive?

We then reach **Part C: Training activities**, the section of the book we think you may return to the most. Here you will find 50 ideas, many of which will be new to you and some of which you may have seen or used before but never thought about in detail. This is the really practical part of the book, where you can get stuck in and try something new. You will find activities that suit your personality or that work for your audience, and some that won't – at least not today. We have tried or observed each and every idea.

**Part D: Evaluating and reflecting on your training and developing yourself as a trainer** gives you the tools and opportunity to be honest with yourself with regard to your own training. We asked you earlier in the book to think about good and bad experiences: well, what would others say about you? What are the indicators that show you quickly how well your training is going? What tells you later if a training session went well? What might you do differently next time?

We will look at different means of *evaluating* your training. This includes both immediate feedback and considering how to measure and understand the impact weeks or even months into the future. We will help you learn to deal with both positive and negative feedback.

Often you may find that someone else *observes* your training sessions. This might be for quality control, out of curiosity or because you are considered an expert. What does it feel like to be observed? How can you get the most out of it? And what's the best approach to observing others?

Lastly, we will give you some ideas for what to do next and where to seek further advice. From our perspective, professional development is ongoing and continuous: the 'C' in CPD. How should you set and maintain your own standards? How can you sense if you are getting into bad habits? How can you keep your knowledge up to date? How can you ensure you remain a reflective practitioner? How has *The Trainer Toolkit* helped you?

Throughout the book you will find some **common features**. In each chapter we begin with a brief overview of the contents and conclude with a checklist. We have brought all the checklists together at the end of the book for your convenience. Parts A, B and D include anecdotes from our own practice and some moments for you to reflect on your experiences. And you will also discover some useful tables, diagrams and pictures of training in context.

We are confident you will find lots to engage with in *The Trainer Toolkit*.

## BOARDING PASS

Before we invite you to open your toolkit, here's an initial reflective activity for you. We call it the *Boarding Pass*. Take a look at Figure 0.1 and rate yourself against each statement. When you have done this, keep your answers somewhere handy. At the end of the book, when you have read it and perhaps tried out some of the ideas and activities, we are going to ask you to do the same activity again for your *Landing Card*.

Read the statements and circle the number that best describes your confidence level. We have phrased the statements to encourage you to think about your experiences so far. *Be honest* and remember there are no right or wrong answers. Rate yourself from 0 to 3 with the highest number meaning the highest confidence.

| | I feel confident that I . . . | | | | |
|---|---|---|---|---|---|
| 1 | can plan a workshop to meet its stated objectives. | 0 | 1 | 2 | 3 |
| 2 | can prepare a range of suitable materials to engage and challenge my audience. | 0 | 1 | 2 | 3 |
| 3 | maximise the environment in which I am working to help my audience in their learning. | 0 | 1 | 2 | 3 |
| 4 | use a variety of presentation techniques to assist in the delivery of my topic. | 0 | 1 | 2 | 3 |
| 5 | understand how to encourage my audience to be active learners in the workshop. | 0 | 1 | 2 | 3 |
| 6 | can adapt the teaching and learning approaches I use for my audience according to their needs. | 0 | 1 | 2 | 3 |
| 7 | can ask, answer and encourage the use of questions. | 0 | 1 | 2 | 3 |
| 8 | know how to manage the behaviour and mindset of a diverse group of adults. | 0 | 1 | 2 | 3 |
| 9 | can help my audience to consider how to put into practice what they have learnt from the workshop. | 0 | 1 | 2 | 3 |
| 10 | have the tools to reflect on what went well and how I could improve my training even more. | 0 | 1 | 2 | 3 |

**Figure 0.1** Boarding Pass

# PART A
# SETTING THE SCENE

# 1

# PROFESSIONAL DEVELOPMENT

## KEY WORDS IN THIS CHAPTER

- reflection
- professional
- development
- participants
- motivation

- viewpoint
- course
- outcomes
- training

## IN THIS CHAPTER YOU WILL:

- reflect upon your own experiences of professional development;
- consider the characteristics of effective professional development;
- understand the different reasons participants reflect positively, or not, upon their experiences of professional development;
- observe professional development from a variety of viewpoints.

# REFLECTING ON YOUR OWN PROFESSIONAL DEVELOPMENT

## WHAT DOES PROFESSIONAL DEVELOPMENT LOOK LIKE IN SCHOOLS?

Before we begin thinking about how to train other teachers and education professionals we must first consider what 'professional development' could look like in our own contexts.

Professionalism is not a fixed set of rules or procedures. Professional development enables you to change yourself, to have professional agency and autonomy.

Professional development is something we all do. When we do it on our own, professional development depends on us reflecting with purpose on our practice.

This may happen when we:

- read a book, article or blog;
- watch a YouTube clip;
- observe a lesson but from a distance;
- keep a journal;
- write a thesis for a Master's degree or doctorate.

However, a lot of professional development happens with other people, either with a colleague or as a group during face-to-face training. In each case, our active engagement, communication and interaction with others helps us to think about our practice.

Such opportunities could include:

- attending a one-day course;
- being part of a 20-minute staff meeting;
- engaging with 13 half-day sessions over a nine-month period;
- having one-to-one coaching;
- listening to a keynote;
- attending a book club;
- observing a lesson.

## SO, WHAT MAKES PROFESSIONAL DEVELOPMENT EFFECTIVE?

Effective professional development has the power to change your practice and your attitudes. It enables you to bring about that change yourself. Effective professional development will be dependent on many variables, including the mode, duration, style and person delivering or receiving it.

## BUT WHAT DO YOU CONSIDER EFFECTIVE PROFESSIONAL DEVELOPMENT TO BE?

- Is it the acquisition of new knowledge?
- Is it the sharing of knowledge?
- Is it the opportunity to engage in some task or activity?
- Is it the reassurance that you are doing everything right?
- Is it more to do with the room, refreshments or people and less to do with the content, tasks or outcomes?
- Is it the opportunity to network with colleagues?
- Is it all of the above?

## TAKE A MOMENT

Can you remember a professional development event that was a really positive experience for you? What was it that made it memorable?

What about a professional development event that was not particularly positive? What was different about this one compared to the previous?

## GOOD EXPERIENCES

We are sure we can all recall an example of a professional development event that we considered to be a success. However, this judgement is subjective, so it depends on what you consider the role of professional development to be.

Often a good experience can be just one moment during a professional development event. For example, you may think of an idea, engage in an activity or have a conversation with someone else which causes you to reflect.

Here are some of the most frequent reasons that our participants have suggested when explaining why a professional development event was good:

- friendly trainer;
- menu and/or venue;
- feeling relaxed;
- made me think;
- impact on learners;
- challenged;
- opportunity to reflect;
- content matched pre-course outline;
- empowered.

A few years ago I was encouraged to attend some training. When I entered the room, I got the feeling it was going to be pitched at ideas I already felt comfortable with, and wondered if it would be worth me staying. I think my face must have given away my feelings, because the trainer came over immediately.

He encouraged me to stay and, after not very long, I was glad I did. Not only did I soon discover that I did in fact have plenty to learn, but much of this learning came from my interactions with the other participants. Even if they might have had less experience than me, many were often more expert. I was also able to see more clearly in the light of their ideas and comments the knowledge and habits – both good and bad – I'd picked up over the years.

At the end of the workshop, I thanked the trainer for opening my mind and for facilitating a session where we all felt comfortable to share, regardless of our experience and expertise. Many of the skills I picked up from this one workshop have positively affected me as a trainer today. And many of the participants remain firm friends.

## BAD EXPERIENCES

Just as we can recall plenty of good experiences, we are certain we can also remember those professional development events that could have been better.

We've all been to training courses which we didn't like. But why is that?

I remember a course when I was a newly qualified teacher. The whole science department had to go to the local training centre for a course *on key skills. Thirty minutes into the course, we were all annoyed, and the more questions we asked, the more frustrated we got.*

*So what had gone wrong?*

*First, our presenter didn't understand what he was trying to teach. Key skills was a government initiative, and he didn't understand how they differed from a previous initiative on skills. Because of this, we felt like we were wasting our time.*

*Second, he had simply chosen to give us a PowerPoint presentation. We did not have professional respect for him. He was supposed to be a trainer, and he was using methods which we as teachers were discouraged from using.*

*But finally, he was up against it from the start. We all knew each other and building a relationship with such a tight-knit group was always going to be a challenge unless he'd really thought about it in advance. There was one positive: I knew how children felt when not taught well!*

Considering the professional development events that the three of us have attended, here are some of our thoughts about why an event may be 'less than good':

- trainer not well prepared;
- room layout not helpful;
- lots of activities but little substance;
- not enough resources to go around;
- pace of event too slow;
- lack of clarity;
- lack of purpose;
- lack of objectives;
- lack of challenge;
- lack of time to reflect;
- I/we were not in the right frame of mind;
- trainer was ineffectual.

## YOUR OWN EXPERIENCES OF PROFESSIONAL DEVELOPMENT

As teachers we have very high expectations. It is our job! However, we often apply these high expectations when attending training sessions and engaging with professional development. We have come to realise that during any training session there are aspects that we enjoy more than others – both as a participant and as a trainer. It is important not to taint the whole training session with those moments that are not so positive (whatever the reason) but to remain focused on the purpose of the professional development.

## TAKE A MOMENT

Make a list of what you particularly like in a training session.

Think about the activities, the room layout, how much listening and talking you are asked to do, whether it is an active or passive session, etc.

Look at Table 1.1. Which elements do you consider to be the most important in affecting how participants engage with professional development? Can you put the 21 elements in order of importance?

**Table 1.1**    Different elements of training sessions

| Elements of training sessions | Number of importance |
| --- | --- |
| Friendly trainer | |
| Comfortable venue | |
| Acquisition of new knowledge | |
| Opportunities to discuss and network with colleagues | |
| Water provided on the tables | |
| Experienced trainer | |
| Friendly participants | |
| Opportunities given to feel valued | |
| Activities and tasks that I can use with immediate effect | |
| Light refreshments provided with tea/coffee | |
| Training that makes me think | |
| Training finishes earlier than advertised time | |
| Active learning features throughout | |
| Opportunities given to reflect | |
| Lunch includes a dessert | |
| Current habitual practice is challenged | |
| Useful handouts | |
| Pre-course tasks set and used in the session | |
| Trainer looks and dresses professionally | |
| Pens and paper are provided | |
| An evaluation of the training is expected | |

Participants may judge a training session to be positive (or negative) based on elements other than the content of the session. As a trainer this is hard, particularly as these aspects (such as the venue or the refreshments) may be out of your control! We are sure we have all attended training sessions where we can remember the delicious cake or the free pen we were given, not so much about the actual content of the session! We will look more closely at this in the next chapter of the book. As a trainer, it is important to be aware of *all* the needs of your participants, which may not be anything to do with the content, materials and delivery of the session.

Last year a colleague and I attended a mathematics symposium. I was particularly excited because an international speaker was booked for the opening plenary and I had wanted to hear him speak for some time. The symposium itself was housed in a historic building which I was yet to visit and so this added to my growing level of anticipation for the event.

I arrived early, got a seat near the front, ensured that my notebook and pen were ready, and prepared myself to be filled with amazing ideas, thoughts and experiences that I would be able to use in future training sessions.

The keynote started well, and I was reassured that, five minutes in, the next fifty-five were going to be equally fulfilling. I was disappointed. I barely made any notes (very unlike me) and felt my mind wandering to take in the beautiful building, but not the content material of the keynote.

At the end of the hour I turned to my colleague, who, before I could speak, enthused about the 'amazing keynote'. I was surprised, and yet it made me realise that we all respond differently to the professional development we receive.

For me, the symposium had not been a waste of time. Quite the opposite. It made me reflect on why I had not been engaged or as excited as perhaps I had anticipated, and so while my mathematical knowledge had not been challenged, my knowledge of being a trainer had.

## TOOLKIT CHECKLIST

When planning your training course, you can now ask yourself the following questions.

- Have I reflected on any recent training I have attended and considered what I can do with what I observed?
- Have I considered the different styles/modes of delivery I have observed and what might be appropriate for the next training session I deliver?
- Have I reminded myself about what professional development means to me and to others?

# 2

# KNOWING YOUR AUDIENCE

## KEY WORDS IN THIS CHAPTER

- audience
- member
- individual
- needs

- rapport
- baggage
- culture

## IN THIS CHAPTER YOU WILL:

- consider who is in your audience;
- discuss what their expectations are;
- think about what might get in the way of their learning;
- learn how to look after your audience's needs.

To be a trainer, we need an audience.

Our audience may be small or large. We may know some of our audience or we may be meeting them for the first time. Some may have a more senior status than us, others less. Some members of our audience might be friendly, others could be hostile.

Each member of the audience is there to learn, and each member of the audience is an individual. Our audience is not one homogenised set of people: they each have their own experiences, expertise, filters, insights, touch points and triggers. And each individual will be interpreting what you have to say in their own way.

The challenge as a trainer is to move away from thinking about yourself and instead think about how to connect with your audience, whatever their individual starting positions.

# WHO IS IN YOUR AUDIENCE?

There can be a wide range of reasons why people are attending your training session. Let's put them into two main categories.

*Personal* – as a participant I want to:

- improve my knowledge or skills;
- prepare for my new job or role;
- have a day out of school;
- catch up with old friends;
- meet my trainer idol!

*Professional* – as a participant I want to:

- improve my students' learning;
- improve my students' exam results;
- get answers or find quick fixes;
- fulfil the conditions of my employment, whereby I need to complete a specific number of hours of development;
- obtain a certificate or qualification.

However, many participants in a training session in fact give little thought to what they want to get out of it or why they are there.

This can be because:

- they have been sent by their school or line manager without a particular purpose or without being briefed;
- training has 'come to town', so they are taking advantage of the opportunity, regardless of the topic;
- they are simply too busy to think that far ahead.

# NEEDS ANALYSIS

How can you get to know your audience's needs? Well, here are two simple ways.

First, *do your prep* in advance of the training session. If you are training colleagues in your school, you will already have a good understanding of the people who will be attending, their reasons for being there and their likely attitude. But don't assume you know. Check the list of participants and imagine yourself in their shoes. What is their entry point? What is the gap in their knowledge or skills that you are seeking to fill? What might they expect to take away?

Secondly, *communicate*. By far the best way to get to know your audience is to talk and listen to them. This is especially important if the participants are completely new to you, as it also helps to break the ice if you start chatting with them as they arrive for the training session. If you have limited opportunity for this beforehand but time permits at the start of the session, ask each participant in turn either to share their expectations out loud or on a piece of paper.

*Even before I am about to give a presentation to a large audience, I try to get to know some of the people who will be sitting in front of me. This way I will have some friendly faces to acknowledge as I arrive on stage, and may even be able to reference in my presentation what they said to me. It feels then like the rest of the audience quickly gets on your side: they know you care about who they are and what they want from you.*

*The audience for a training session is usually much smaller, so you can often greet every single person when they come into the room. I some-times take brief notes – maybe just a word or two – on each individual. I then extend this more formally when the training session begins by inviting them to write their objectives or specific questions anonymously on a sticky note. I usually post these on the wall and keep finding moments to look at them to gauge if I am meeting expectations and answering questions. In this way I feel much closer to my partici-pants' needs, and they have that impression too.*

By preparing carefully for your audience and communicating directly with them, you should soon have a broad answer to each of the following five questions.

1.  What does your audience already know?
2.  How diverse are their starting points?
3.  What is their mindset – do they appear open or closed to new ideas?
4.  How ready are they to engage with learning?
5.  What do they want to know?

And it is this last question that remains the key to successful training. Both when preparing and delivering training, keep thinking: what would it be like to be in your own audience?

As a fellow trainer once put it, each individual in your audience is tuned to their own radio station: *WII-FM – What's In It For Me?*

## BUILDING RAPPORT

There is a good chance that you will feel nervous at the beginning of a training session, however experienced you are. This is natural, and if you manage it properly, it can stop you from being complacent. As we will see in **Part B**, you can remove a lot of personal and professional obstacles or challenges by creating your own conditions for success early on. This includes helping your audience get ready to engage and learn.

Building rapport is about putting other people at ease. It is about minimising differences and removing barriers. Many of your participants could be nervous too. It might be their first time at a training session, they might be new to the group, they might be far from home. Reach out to them to listen to and appreciate their hopes and fears. Break down barriers by helping them get to know each other as well as you: share something about yourself as a person.

You may be self-conscious, especially when you first meet your training participants. From your perspective as a trainer, this can most often manifest itself in nervousness, but also in arrogance if you seek to prove yourself. To turn this around, instead try to be audience-conscious. The training is, after all, about them rather than about you. Find common ground in the training room and use this to everyone's advantage.

When I undertook my first training courses abroad, I did two one-day courses in different schools. I worked very hard to prepare but didn't expect them to go brilliantly well (after all, I was a rookie!). I finished the day at the first school and was really pleased. Everyone was happy, they all said how much they'd enjoyed it and how much they'd learnt from it. They all participated and the energy in the room was really fantastic!

So, imagine my disappointment when a few days later things turned out very differently. It started badly because we were delayed in traffic, so we arrived at the venue with just 30 minutes to set up. Unfortunately, the head teacher wanted to offer us tea and biscuits and it would have been very rude to refuse. As such, I walked into the training room five minutes before the start of the course.

*Because of this, I hadn't had time to put out all the resources, or even to check all the resources were there· It made me feel unprepared; the effect on my confidence I'm sure was noticeable, and I know that this affected the confidence the audience had in me· But I had already made another mistake· I'd assumed that what would work in one school would work in another·*

*It didn't – for several reasons· First, I hadn't researched the school, so I had not tailored the activities to the teachers in front of me· Second, I'd not built in a chance for the audience members to share their expertise; this was particularly important for this audience because they came from some of the most prestigious schools in the country and expected their expertise to be recognised· Finally, I had assumed (without knowing it) that participation would lead to learning· It didn't· Since then, I've really understood the need for participants to reflect, and reflect together, in order to make sense of and apply the key messages of the course to think about their own classrooms·*

## BAGGAGE

As a trainer, you will often find yourself tripping over laptop cases and rucksacks, but there is another type of baggage in the room that is less visible but just as hazardous.

### TAKE A MOMENT

When you last attended a training session, what else was on your mind? How easy was it to switch off and focus on what was in the room? How often, for example, were you checking your phone? And how do you think it affected how much you got out of the session?

We can divide baggage into the same two categories we saw above, although there is not necessarily a correlation between the two lists.

*Personal* – due to:

- work-life balance;
- difficulties at home;
- stress about something that has happened and is unresolved;
- anxiety about something unrelated that will or may happen later;
- how difficult it was to reach the training venue.

*Professional* – because participants feel:

- angry about what their school/exam board/state is demanding of them;
- aggrieved about a decision – for example, an exam grade they disagree with;
- they have never previously gained much from training sessions;
- they are superior to you in terms of experience or expertise;
- they could do a better job than you as the trainer.

You as a trainer may of course also be suffering from any one or all of the above. Somehow you will need to remain professional and set your own baggage to one side. Once again, your focus needs to be your audience and their needs.

There is, of course, little you can do to influence many of the items on the personal list. The point here, though, is to be conscious that members of your audience may not always be entirely focused on what is going on in your training session. All the same, one of your aims is to engage them in such a way that they can leave their troubles behind, at least for a while. Value their time and contributions – and, if they need it, also give them a moment to defuse!

How you deal with the professional baggage will depend on who you are working for. If you are delivering training on behalf of your school, make sure you feel secure about policy. If you disagree with what the school is demanding and asking you to talk about, work through these differences before the training session rather than during it. You may feel more comfortable inviting a colleague to co-facilitate with you about a particularly contentious point.

If you are working for an exam board, the state or another organisation, again be clear with your information and, if need be, your justifications. Training on behalf of an awarding body that sets and grades examinations is specialist work. You really need to know your topic in depth and do your research – set yourself up for success. This is your chance to talk with clarity and shine light on an area which may for some time have been problematic for your participants.

It is quite possible that members of your audience will have many more years' experience than you, in their role, at the school or in education. But they are not necessarily more expert than you – it is a fallacy that experience directly leads to expertise. You should not allow yourself to feel like an imposter. The fact that you are the trainer should mean that, if you have carefully analysed their needs, you have something of value to give to all members of the audience. And if you have read this book (unlike them), you should have all the tools to deliver it!

# CULTURE

One of the great things about being a trainer is the number of different people you get to meet. You can learn a lot from your participants and cross-pollinate with another audience that you work with at a later date. You will find yourself doing this with regard to ideas and also culture. Schools, organisations and companies have different ways of working and interacting; the same, of course, goes for people who live, have grown up in or spent time in other countries.

You will find, for example, that there may be diverse attitudes to:

- how the trainer is perceived;
- how your audience listens, contributes and gives feedback;
- the use of mobile phones during training.

If you are going somewhere new – be it an educational institution or another part of the world – again, do your prep. Know in advance if something is likely to offend or appeal. Learning a few words of the local language, if you are travelling, can quickly help build a rapport. If you have time, visit the local surroundings and attune yourself to what is happening in the news. Steer clear, though, of talking about anything that may turn your audience against you!

We have given you a taster of the sorts of things to look out for when thinking about your audience. We will develop many of these in greater detail in the next few chapters.

## TOOLKIT CHECKLIST

When planning your training course, you can now ask yourself the following questions.

- Have I thought about my audience?
- Have I considered their individual needs?
- Have I understood that my audience might have different ways of working?

# 3

# WORKING WITH ADULTS

## KEY WORDS IN THIS CHAPTER

- adults
- learning
- theories
- traits

- motivation
- difficult
- facilitating
- take-away

### IN THIS CHAPTER YOU WILL:

- consider how training adults is different to teaching school students;
- reflect on different theories of adult learning;
- think about how to motivate adults;
- begin to recognise your own training traits.

It is likely that all of your professional training to date has been focused on supporting the students you teach. Some of the skills and techniques you employ to teach your students can be transferred to training adults. But not all of them!

There are several factors which contribute to these differences:

- adults (mostly) choose to attend training, while students have no choice;
- the adults in your audience are also your peers, so you need to treat them as equals and yet support them in their learning;

- your adult audience is potentially more critical, because they too are educators (of students);
- time is precious and so unlike students, who often enjoy time away from their lessons, adults can feel anxious that they are losing valuable teaching time;
- you may not know your audience (or at least they may not know you in this capacity), so you need to establish credibility and earn respect.

## THEORIES OF ADULT LEARNING

There are many different theories about how adults learn. We will outline a few here, but you will need to decide which model fits with your style of training. While the three of us have similar techniques, we are also very different trainers.

Thomas Guskey (2002) is well known for his theories on professional development. While he is an advocate of adult training, he also reminds us that reviews of professional development consistently point out that most programmes are ineffective. He believes this is because:

1. the programme does not take into account what motivates teachers to engage in professional development;
2. the programme does not take into account the process by which change in teachers typically occurs.

We will discuss motivation later on in this chapter.

Guskey's second point is interesting because it relates to the process of teacher change. We may aspire to change participants' beliefs and attitudes about something during the training session, which will then lead to a change in classroom practice which will ultimately result in improved outcomes for students. But Guskey suggests that the sequence may in fact be as shown in Figure 3.1.

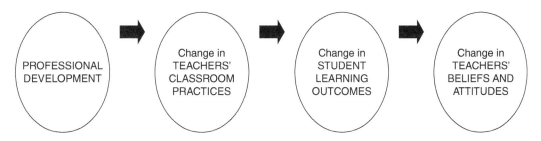

**Figure 3.1** The sequence of change following professional development

In other words, participants attend training, they change their practice as a result (not because they know it is going to work, but because they are confident to take a risk and hope it will), students' learning outcomes improve and only *then* do the participants' beliefs and attitudes change.

Another researcher, Malcolm Knowles (1984), talks about four principles for adult learning.

1.  Adults need to be involved in the planning and evaluation of their instruction.
2.  Experience (including the mistakes we make) provides the basis for the learning activities.
3.  Adults are most interested in learning subjects that have immediate relevance and impact for their job or personal life.
4.  Adult learning is problem-centred rather than content-oriented.

More recently, Bridget Clay and David Weston (2018) discussed five reasons why adult learning can be tricky.

1.  *Confirmation bias.* Because our brains are quicker to adopt familiar or new ideas that support existing thinking, one single session is rarely enough to shift thinking. We therefore tend to ignore or rapidly forget unfamiliar ideas and block out or reject things that contradict what we already believe.
2.  *Sunk cost bias.* We will often resist change, even if the new idea or resource is objectively better. This is because we like to hold onto things that we have worked hard to achieve.
3.  *Dunning-Kruger effect.* This is the result when we confuse enthusiasm for experience. As a participant we may hear an idea, listen to a speech or watch a video that was previously confusing but suddenly it makes sense. We can mistake this excitement for expertise.
4.  *Halo effect.* This relates to how we perceive the people we are listening to. If we like a person, or if they are charismatic and impress us, we tend to believe them, but if we take a personal dislike to them, we can be quick to dismiss their ideas.
5.  *Fundamental attribution error.* We are resistant to criticism. So, for example, if a colleague or a trainer says something negative, then we stop believing their ideas.

It is quite easy to spot these biases in other people, but we all inherently have these wired into the way we think. As a trainer, it is important to look out for them and not be afraid to admit they exist, in both our participants and ourselves.

Remember that a group of adults are almost certainly going to have different prior knowledge and starting points in relation to the course objectives. It is really important to find out some information from your audience before you begin. **Part C** offers ideas for icebreakers to establish the level of experience you have in the room.

## TRAINER TRAITS

Being a good trainer is about being able to recognise your own style and developing it. It is always useful (essential even) to watch other trainers train. You will begin to notice their training techniques and reflect on whether you can incorporate them in your own training style. However, it is also important to note that you can't just copy them. For example, a trainer who uses a lot of humour in their delivery appears to do this with ease, yet it is likely to be their personality that helps them to do so. If this is not within your usual 'make-up' your participants will notice!

## TAKE A MOMENT

What do you think your training traits may be?
  If someone had to describe how you are as a trainer, what might they say?

Have a look at the words below. Which would you like to be associated with as a trainer? Which do you think are appropriate to you? Can you choose five that really exemplify your training traits?

| | | | | |
|---|---|---|---|---|
| friendly | thoughtful | sensible | sparkly | reflective |
| creative | inspirational | humorous | knowledgeable | adaptable |
| challenging | responsive | strict | confident | enthusiastic |
| relaxed | practical | authoritative | approachable | personable |

We decided to put these training traits to the test! To begin, the three of us chose five traits that we thought were representative of ourselves when training. We then challenged one another to choose five traits they would use to describe each of us when training. You will see that there are some similarities but also some differences.

*Alison selected: sparkly, enthusiastic, confident, inspirational, reflective.*

*Paul and Mark (between them) chose: sparkly, enthusiastic, confident, knowledgeable, practical.*

*Paul selected: sensible, humorous, confident, authoritative, personable.*

*Alison and Mark (between them) chose: sensible, humorous, confident, personable, friendly, relaxed, thoughtful, adaptable.*

*Mark selected: friendly, enthusiastic, personable, thoughtful, relaxed.*

*Paul and Alison (between them) chose: enthusiastic, thoughtful, humorous, practical, sensible, knowledgeable, reflective, creative, inspirational, approachable.*

We enjoyed doing this activity, and it created a professional conversation about the traits we think we have and the traits we would like to have!

## MOTIVATING ADULT LEARNERS

As **Chapter 2** outlined, knowing and understanding your audience is key. However, even if your adult learners arrive with some 'baggage', your role as a trainer is to be empathetic, but then to enable and encourage them to engage in your training.

There are many factors which can either enable or disable motivation, some of which may be beyond your control. One way of looking at motivation is Maslow's (1954) hierarchy of needs (Figure 3.2).

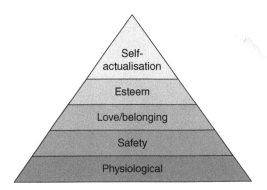

**Figure 3.2**   Maslow's hierarchy of needs

If your participants are cold or hungry (physiological), they are less likely to be motivated to learn. Equally if they do not feel that the training environment is safe (both physically and emotionally) they may be withdrawn and struggle to feel engaged and motivated. You may not be able to help with all needs, but checking that your participants are comfortable (for example, the temperature of the room, if seating arrangements are conducive) is an easy task. And of course, never underestimate the power that providing biscuits and sweets provides!

*When I am delivering mathematics training I am always aware that I may have participants in the room who do not feel very confident with the subject and may even associate mathematics with right and wrong answers in tests and exams.*

*I try to put them at their ease, in a relaxed way, by telling them that today there will be no tests and, furthermore, I expect everyone to work with at least one other person. While a few adults may be disappointed not to show off their mathematical skills, the majority visibly relax and settle down to the tasks at hand.*

Another way to think about motivation is to focus on extrinsic or intrinsic motivation.

Within a training environment, *extrinsic* motivation is driven by external rewards, such as the number of activities people take away with them, whether biscuits/lunch/sweets are provided or whether they are seen by the other participants to be the most knowledgeable or experienced. This type of motivation arises from outside the individual.

*Intrinsic* motivation originates from within the individual. This is more concerned with the pursuit of knowledge. It is personally rewarding. Rather than involving a particular goal, you engage with it because you enjoy it. This type of motivation is more longitudinal, in that you are more focused on learning and improving.

How you choose to motivate adults is up to you, but here are a few *trade secrets*!

1.  Try to say hello to everyone before you start the session. This helps participants to feel noticed and builds relationships. In return they will feel more inclined to participate.
2.  Ask for examples and comments throughout the training session. This enables participants to feel valued and shows that you are not simply 'the expert'.
3.  When taking participants' contributions, add a few personal comments too. For example, 'I really like that idea' or 'That's an interesting way to think about it.' This offers praise to the person giving the feedback (which we all like) but also helps to motivate others to contribute.
4.  Move around the room during the session if possible. Standing at the front can appear 'teacher like' whereas standing, sitting or kneeling in different places allows you to engage with more participants.

5.  Try not to have all the answers immediately. This can be off-putting and demotivating, especially if some of your participants are on a learning curve. So, practise pausing and then asking other participants what they think, before giving your view.
6.  Towards the end of the session, offer a summary of what you have covered. This helps remind participants of the quantity and breadth of the training. Next, ask people to suggest their favourite part, or what they are going to take away. Even if a few people were feeling slightly demotivated, this exercise helps to halt these thoughts and focuses attention on next steps.
7.  At the beginning of the session, you will have adopted a more authoritative persona, simply because you are leading the session. However, the skill is to begin to transfer this position of power to your participants, so that by the end of the session they feel empowered and motivated.

Motivating adults does not mean that you have to agree with all of their ideas and contributions. Ultimately, your role as a trainer is to enable your audience to improve their knowledge and skills. While it is a natural human emotion to want to be liked by your adult peers, this will not ultimately gain you respect as a trainer. Part of your role is to offer challenge, and opportunities for reflection. However, remember that the training environment is not the school playground and areas of conflict are welcomed and used to shape thinking rather than as grounds for disagreement.

## DEALING WITH DIFFICULT ADULTS

There may be occasions when you do need to manage the adults in the room. Let us look at a few scenarios and offer some suggestions.

Scenario:   One of your participants strongly disagrees with something you have said.

Advice:   Thank them for their contribution, acknowledge that your viewpoints are different but stick to your message.

Scenario:   A group of adults continue their conversation when you are talking.

Advice:   Don't talk louder! Pause and wait until you have their attention before you continue. If it persists, gently but firmly ask them to respect others by pausing their conversation until you have finished.

Scenario:   One or two participants refuse to join in with their group or any of the tasks set.

Advice:   As you circulate around the room, stop at the table with these delegates and try to ascertain (indirectly, through observation, listening) why they are not engaged. If appropriate ask them how they are finding the session and what their thoughts are regarding the specific task. Don't be offended if they respond negatively – you can't always win everyone round!

Scenario:   A few participants are always the first (and loudest) to respond when you ask for feedback.

Advice:   Use strategies such as 'Envoys' and 'Rainbow' (Activity 18 in Part C) to deflect away from immediate whole-group discussion. Alternatively, target specific people for feedback.

Scenario:   One or two participants are relentless in asking questions.

Advice:   Thank them for their questions, respond if it is appropriate but alternatively 'store' them somewhere to answer later. Often it is helpful to have a place (for example, a questions board) where participants can write their questions.

## FACILITATING ACTIVE LEARNING WITH ADULTS

Active learning is a process by which people construct their own knowledge rather than it simply being delivered to them. We use active learning as a key pedagogical tool in the classroom so why not also use it in training?

However, it is also a strategy that is misunderstood. Often the word 'active' is misinterpreted to mean physically active rather than cognitively active.

As teachers and educational professionals, we do like the sound of our own voices! We are also appreciative of an attentive audience and so we can fall into the trap, both as a teacher and as a trainer, of talking too much. Of course, there are times when we do need to talk. As a trainer it is important to notice if your audience is more passive than active and build in tasks to address this.

Here are a few tips to help your training include active learning opportunities.

- Consider how to arrange the furniture so that it enables participants to talk easily with one another.
- At any point, even if it is not planned, ask participants to talk to each other for a couple of minutes.
- Choose rich tasks that will enable participants to think and make choices so you are allowing them to build up their own knowledge. (For example, 'Diamond Nine' (Activity 21 in **Part C**) activities work well here.)
- Use both questions and statements so that participants have a chance to think about the answer before you tell them.
- Use mistakes and misconceptions to provoke discussion.
- Remind participants that thinking, and thinking harder, is key to learning.
- Use a variety of pedagogical techniques in your training (for example, designing a poster, key words on sticky notes, six-word headlines (Activity 39 in **Part C**)), and after task completion, talk about how the pedagogical choice you made either enabled or disabled learning and thinking.

## TAKE A MOMENT

Look at the two photographs below.
   What evidence is there in each picture to show active learning?

**Figure 3.3**   Two contrasting photographs exemplifying active learning

# HELPING ADULTS TO KNOW WHAT TO TAKE AWAY

Attending any form of training, participants will expect to 'take away' something from the session. This may be in a physical form, such as handouts, or it may involve improved thinking and ideas.

Whatever you have decided as the trainer or facilitator, one of the first questions you will get asked is 'Can we have a copy of the slides?' (if you are using a presentation mode of delivery). This is up to you (unless you have been specifically contracted). If you do decide to provide physical copies, think whether it is more appropriate to hand them out at the beginning (so participants can map their notes against the relevant slides) or at the end (as an aide-mémoire, or to use when they disseminate the training to others).

It may be appropriate to encourage your participants to take their own notes, in whatever form they are most comfortable with. We have observed great variety and skill in the notes participants make, ranging from beautiful mind maps, logical, organised notes, reflective journals and 'back of the envelope' jottings.

How participants record their thinking is personal and subjective. You will need to build in opportunities during the session to allow participants to stop, reflect and record any points which are pertinent to them.

*I recently delivered a training session on 'Mathematical Literacy'. I had chosen not to provide slides and informed the participants of this at the beginning.*

*After the session I was chatting to colleagues and was delighted to find that a few had recorded their notes through drawings (Figure 3.4). It made me wonder: had I given out slides, would they have still recorded the information in this way?*

You may choose to issue boarding passes (see **Introduction**) and landing cards (see **Chapter 14**) at the beginning and end of your session, just as we are providing in this book! The landing card in particular helps participants to reflect on the training, review what they have learnt and consider what they need to do next.

**Figure 3.4**   Participant's notes from a training session

Sketches reproduced with permission of Rachel West

Alternatively, you might choose to ask participants for one of their key 'take-aways'. Give people a few minutes to decide what they will offer (this also helps to set the expectation that you are assuming everyone will contribute). Take a look at **Chapter 11** in **Part C** for more suggestions on how to do this. It is always surprising how different these comments can be – often it's not what you expect.

Finally, we would encourage you always to provide tasks for participants to do after the training event has finished. You can choose whether to suggest tasks as you are going through the session, or summarise with a list at the end. Either way, you are putting the C into the CPD (*continuing* professional development); in other words, just because the training has finished, the participants' learning has not. It is, of course, up to participants to decide if they wish to complete any of the tasks. Here are a few suggestions you could give to your participants.

- Try out one of the tasks you have used in the training session.
- Chat to a colleague about something that surprised you.
- Follow up on some research that was used.
- Re-read your notes.
- Write a blog about your training experience.

## TOOLKIT CHECKLIST

When planning your training course, you can now ask yourself the following questions.

- Have I switched from thinking as a teacher to working as a trainer?
- Have I reflected on the different theories of adult learning and considered how these might affect my next training session?
- Have I put myself in the participants' shoes and viewed the training from their perspective?
- Have I considered which training traits I might be employing?
- Have I reflected on the different reasons why the participants are attending the training?
- Have I thought how to motivate and empower the participants?

# 4

# DISSEMINATING LEARNING

## KEY WORDS IN THIS CHAPTER

- disseminating
- learning
- cascade
- model

- train-the-trainer
- participants
- resources
- expertise

## IN THIS CHAPTER YOU WILL:

- think about how training can be disseminated and cascaded;
- think about the ways in which training may impact upon your participants;
- learn how to empower your participants to disseminate or cascade their learning.

## THE CASCADE MODEL

Whatever type of professional development you are involved in, the outcomes are going to be disseminated to others. More and more people may be impacted by your training the more it is disseminated. Dissemination may happen in all sorts of ways. It can be as simple as copying the notes and emailing them to colleagues, talking for five minutes in a staff meeting or over coffee, having informal corridor conversations or readjusting action plans as a result of the training.

In the so-called 'train-the-trainer' model, participants' learning may be more formally cas-caded, with each level of teaching staff training the level below it. For example, if you are educating teachers, you hope *they* will learn something, but you also hope their learning outcomes will be disseminated or cascaded to other members of staff or through their class-room practice to influence students' learning.

So, your training may have immediate impact on two levels:

* participants' knowledge, attitudes and skills;
* participants' students' learning outcomes.

But it may also have impact on other levels:

* the wider student body;
* the wider teaching staff;
* departmental policies;
* institutional norms and policies.

Because of this, you need to think not just about the learning of participants in your training room, but also how to help them disseminate their learning to others. You also need to decide at which levels of the cascade to evaluate your training (see **Chapter 12**). Figure 4.1 represents this kind of cascade for teachers training other teachers, with the training eventu-ally impacting on students.

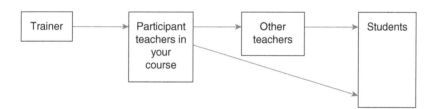

**Figure 4.1**   Cascading training

# THINKING ABOUT IMPACT

Participants in your training course will be different to each other in the following ways.

* Some teachers will always seek out opportunities for growth and will have booked them-selves onto a training course having seen it advertised. They are highly likely to imple-ment what they have learnt in their own practice.
* Some teachers have a very positive attitude to developing their practice. To grow they will attend training courses when prompted by others and participate with a positive attitude depending on who else they are working with. However, perhaps because they are very busy, they seldom do anything with what they have learnt so their classroom practice does not develop.

- Some teachers are reticent and resistant to change. They will try to avoid being involved in professional development and may not participate or have a negative influence on those around them during training. They do not learn and their own practice does not change.

Having delivered training courses for some time, and in many different countries, I suddenly found myself with an unexpected challenge. There were a lot of teachers in one particular course who appeared unwilling to participate and unwilling to think about their practice.

How did I know? It took me over two minutes to get them to be silent at the start of the course so that I could introduce myself. This seemed quite impolite to me and my instinctive reaction to their behaviour assumed they were all resistant to change. I was not looking forward to the day ahead!

Instead of introducing myself, I set them going on the first task by putting instructions on the PowerPoint. As they slowly began work, I chatted to the individual teachers and realised that most of them had been sent on the course, that they did not understand how it was relevant and that many had had to organise extra childcare for their children.

By building positive relationships over the course of the day, making the training relevant and forcing them to think about their own classrooms, it became apparent quickly that they were keen to learn, had left feeling very positive and at least had good intentions to implement the ideas into their practice.

However, even for those teachers whose practice is affected by your training, you may see different levels of adoption.

- Some teachers may simply *imitate* some of the activities you show them, implementing them in precisely the same context as you suggested. For example, let's say you mentioned using graphic organisers in a training course for science teachers, to help students remember the different levels of classification (species, genus, etc.). The participants would replicate such use in their lessons on classification, ignoring any other discussion of their potential during the course.

- Some teachers may take such activities but engage in *horizontal transfer*. For example, using the graphic organiser to help students remember any long lists of unfamiliar words.
- Some teachers may use strategies more *innovatively*. For example, using the graphic organiser approach to help students sequence cause-and-effect relationships across different history lessons.
- Some teachers may have a strong understanding of the theoretical justification behind particular teaching and learning approaches, *and* employ them *reflectively* to secure good learning outcomes and to reflect upon change in other aspects of their practice.

## TAKE A MOMENT

The way in which your training course fits into a wider programme of professional development may influence how teachers respond to it. For example, you may be running a six-week programme with a group of teachers with monthly follow-up meetings, or you may simply have been invited to run a two-hour workshop on a training day.

A teacher's priorities in attending the course may also have an impact.

Think about professional development courses and programmes you have attended. Did the training affect your practice? And to what extent did imitation, innovation or reflective understanding do so?

# EMPOWERING PARTICIPANTS TO DISSEMINATE THEIR LEARNING

Participants in your training may be responsible for disseminating your training when they go back to their departments or their schools. When dissemination goes wrong, the outcomes of the training may not be passed on effectively. This is made worse when teachers simply *tell* other teachers about the training rather than helping them to *think* about the training in relation to their own practice.

*The more you train, the more you will develop your own training style and traits. This can be a hindrance when attending training run by others, which you then need to disseminate to your own audience!*

*(Continued)*

*(Continued)*

*I recently attended a training session which I had been very much look-ing forward to. I knew the two colleagues leading the training and was very excited about their new project. I was keen to learn more and was very much looking forward to cascading it back to my own peer group (with their permission of course).*

*Quite early on I realised that their mode of delivery was completely different to mine. For example, they didn't feel the need to set the scene or offer the big picture and they dropped in literature references, albeit quietly and without key information.*

*I started by jotting down occasional words and phrases but was soon trying to capture verbatim what they were saying. This was a disaster on my part. I stopped, paused and changed tack.*

*I found a new clean page, grabbed a few different coloured pens and began building up a picture of their presentation using a form of mind map (something which I do not default to regularly).*

*By the end of the presentation I had enough information to disseminate back to my own colleagues, but it would take some work on my part to get it into a style that I could use.*

To try to make your participants *think* and so increase the chance they will make other teachers *think* about their practice, adopt the following principles when planning and carry-ing out your training.

- *Avoid* lectures. Participants need to participate. Activities which require discussion with others can really help. Without participation, boredom sets in.
- *Encourage* reflection. Participants should be asked to think about *how* and *why* their new knowledge, skills and abilities could be assimilated into their own classroom practice, and even to think about *whether* the ideas you are presenting are relevant to their own classrooms.
- *Put value* on reinterpretation. When reflecting, participants may adapt what they have learnt so that the outcomes for their classroom are very different to what you suggested. This is good: do not expect a teacher to blindly follow a lesson-recipe – they need to make sense of the ideas for themselves to build them successfully into their practice.
- *Develop* expert knowledge. To help them reflect, share pedagogical and theoretical knowledge. They can use that knowledge to train others.
- Try to *include others* when you plan your training. If you have already talked to your par-ticipants about what they want and how they like to be trained, their learning outcomes will be better secured.

Your aim is to encourage participation, to be sensitive to your participants' context, to foster collaboration, and to make your participants reflect. If you do that, then you will enable participants to disseminate their learning to others as well. If they understand how and why you designed the training as you did, then they will be better able to disseminate that learning to other teachers and educational professionals, and to incorporate the outcomes into their classroom practice.

## TAKE A MOMENT

Table 4.1 may be a useful handout for teachers who are expected to formally cascade their learning to help them plan effectively.

Think about a professional development course you recently delivered or in which you participated, and reflect on how much you (or the trainer) adhered to the principles in the checklist.

**Table 4.1**    Design checklist to help participants cascade their learning

| How does the training course allow participants to: |
| --- |
| • participate, rather than just listen? |
| • make use of their own experience and context? |
| • think and reflect, particularly in response to 'how' and 'why' questions? |
| • collaborate with each other? |
| • receive and make use of expert knowledge? |
| • try out or experience ideas and activities themselves? |
| • apply ideas, for example to their own context? |
| • practise, apply and evaluate what they have learnt during the training session? |
| • ask questions and develop understanding individually with the trainer? |
| • reflect on the aims and purposes of each part of the training course? |

*I once led a team of trainers to go to another country and train teachers to be trainers so that these teachers could, in turn, train other teachers. We had just a week in which to do this, and the second group*

*(Continued)*

*(Continued)*

*of teachers would arrive on days 4 and 5 to be trained by the new trainers!*

*We planned the training in detail, but we knew there were two main variables: (a) did the teachers have the potential to be trainers? (b) did they have sufficient knowledge of the topics they would be training the other teachers about?*

*As we only had three days to train the teachers, we decided to check both variables simultaneously. This meant devising activities that consolidated topic knowledge while demonstrating the skills of being a trainer. We also had to include moments for in-depth reflection to check that the teachers knew both what excellent training looks like and what were the key points in the topics that needed to be passed on to the teachers they would be training. On the third day, we invited each teacher to deliver a showcase, asked them to self-reflect, then gave individual feedback.*

*Many of the teachers proved to be very good at training, and we were able to let them lead sessions on their own at the end of the week. Others were less able, so we asked them to co-facilitate with us or assist instead. It was important for nobody to 'lose face' as all the teachers knew who had been selected as potential trainers.*

*The plan after our week with the new trainers was for them to train even more teachers in other schools throughout their country. We hope that the advice we gave stayed with them and that they were able to continue to evaluate themselves and each other and develop as trainers. At some point in disseminating training you have to let go, but you need to do all you can to think through not only the initial variables but also what will happen next.*

If your participants have to cascade your *training* by running the training course themselves, you can help by:

- sending the resources from the training in editable format to participants;
- including explanatory notes with each PowerPoint slide to share the thinking behind the slide's contents and the ideas presented (if you did talk about the ideas on each slide, it is likely that the participants may not have listened to everything you said);
- including your own planning document, which explains the purpose or learning outcomes of each activity, and how it is designed to achieve that purpose.

In so doing, you are sharing your expertise, both to help them achieve the intended learning outcomes, but also to help them to have the knowledge which enables them to cascade to others. Providing the resources above can also help teachers to cascade your training in other ways:

- observing and providing feedback to teachers;
- supporting teachers in an inquiry/action research programme;
- coaching and mentoring teachers;
- contributing to an improvement process across the department or school;
- contributing to study groups or 'teaching and learning' groups among the staff.

This book is primarily about training. But as you will see from what follows, being a good teacher does not necessarily make you a good trainer, although being a good trainer can help you to become a better teacher. Your participants will need all the help they can get in learning to teach adults and in getting adults to learn, whether in a training course or any of the other points above.

## TOOLKIT CHECKLIST

When planning your training course, you can now ask yourself the following questions.

- Have I considered how participants in my training will disseminate their learning?
- Have I thought about the different levels (students, teachers, departments, whole school) in a school at which my course may have impact?
- Have I designed a training course which will empower participants to cascade their learning?

# PART B

# GETTING READY TO TRAIN

# 5
# PLANNING

## KEY WORDS IN THIS CHAPTER

- planning
- purpose
- objectives
- activities
- modes of delivery
- impact

- template
- timing
- structure
- beginning
- ending

## IN THIS CHAPTER YOU WILL:

- understand the importance of both purpose and objectives;
- explore how to use time effectively in your training sessions;
- consider how to structure and scaffold learning;
- think about how to set the tone with your audience and satisfy their objectives.

Having set the scene in **Part A**, we now move onto the substance of training. In this part of the book, we will look in turn at the materials you could use, how to make the most of the space in which you are training, and the skills you need to communicate. But before we begin, we need a plan.

# PURPOSE AND OBJECTIVES

We all engage in some level of planning in our jobs, but what does it look like in a training context? If you are a teacher, someone may regularly critique your lesson plans. This happens much less when you are a trainer, unless you have been commissioned to write workshop materials. In other words, you are the one who is responsible for getting the plan right and for evaluating properly afterwards whether your plan worked as you intended.

## TAKE A MOMENT

List the ways in which planning a training session might differ from how you plan a lesson. For example, think about the aims, objectives, timings, activities, opportunities for interaction, modes of delivery, structure, language and vocabulary, theoretical references, evaluation.

It is surprising – not just in the context of training – how many people talk about their 'strategies' or 'objectives' and how few actually think properly about the 'purpose' of what they are doing.

Here's one easy mnemonic you could use to help you think about your training session (or indeed, with adaptation, anything else you are planning):

**Table 5.1**   The POST mnemonic

| P | Purpose | Why is this training session taking place? |
|---|---------|--------------------------------------------|
| O | Objective(s) | What do you want to achieve and your participants to learn? |
| S | Strategies | How will you do it? Which activities will you use? |
| T | Tools | Which materials and resources will you need? |

We will be looking at Strategies and Tools in other chapters of this book, so we will just focus on the first two letters of the mnemonic for now.

Imagine you are an experienced examiner who has been asked, as part of a CPD programme, to help other teachers in your school build a greater understanding of assessment. You are planning a one-day course for a group of teachers.

The *purpose* of the training day in this example is very clearly 'to improve a group of teachers' understanding of assessment'. The main focus of your set of core *objectives* will be aspects of assessment.

Don't forget as well that, before you can start talking seriously about assessment, you need to get to know your group and let them get to know you. You also, importantly, need to gauge the level of understanding the group of teachers already has. There is little point in pitching the level of training too high or too low.

You should build relationships with your participants as early as you can, as well as set some shared ground rules agreed by all. The participants need to feel they can trust you and that the training will be worth their while, as we discussed in **Chapter 3**. A good way to think about this is in terms of *empowerment*: in what ways are you going to transform their thinking and their practice to enable them to be better at what they do?

## TAKE A MOMENT

Think about a recent training session you attended. What was its *purpose*? Did it succeed?

You can also, of course, identify the purpose of articles you read or presentations you hear. To what extent is the purpose clear? How much thought has the writer or speaker given to this?

Think of another training session you have recently attended. Can you list the trainer's three main *objectives*?

You may alternatively want to reflect on a meeting you were invited to. Was the meeting properly planned? Were there clear objectives? The same principles apply.

And how will you know your starting point and be able to evaluate the impact of your training? In the opening session you could ask some closed questions to test your participants' level of knowledge. A good example of this is a trainer working for an assessment organisation who wants to know how much of the syllabus documentation teachers have read. You could then push further with some basic, but more open, questions about their understanding of the topic. If you have the facility to do so, ask these questions in a pre-course questionnaire.

Now think about what else you could reasonably cover in session one. For our example about understanding assessment, this might include looking at who we assess, why we assess, how we assess and when we assess. Depending on the knowledge of the group, this may be sufficient. Do not overpromise – less can be more, and too much information can quickly lose its value.

Regardless of how many objectives you decide to set for each of your sessions and for the whole training course, the key point again is to remember *why* you are delivering the training in the first place. If you keep this in mind, it keeps you focused.

Trainers – especially those working as external consultants – are usually given a contract which sets out what you need to do in order to be paid. It is essential to establish what the client wants. If you are not given the purpose for the training and its objectives are not obvious, it might be a good idea to ask the question. You may in fact need to help your client shape the purpose. In this way, you are far more likely to meet expectations, and feel more at ease with what you are doing.

It is good practice to establish a shared understanding of the purpose of the training and the objectives at the beginning of each session. You should also review them at appropriate moments, checking throughout that the training is matching the participants' needs. This is particularly true if the training session is a long one or extends over a period of time.

*I once attended a crushingly expensive workshop where we, a very large group of senior managers, were being asked to devise a list of adjectives to describe our organisation's 'values'· The room was lavish; the stationery was unlike anything even Alison would have seen before; the bottles of water and confectionery on every table were top of the range·*

*It was clear what our objective was – to agree on some words – but why? Well, we certainly weren't told at the beginning of the session, and we weren't told at the end· The cynical among us could only assume it was because this kind of exercise was simply 'trendy' and the trainer had copied it from elsewhere without really knowing why they were using it·*

*And so, in the first instance, it was really hard to take the poorly designed workshop activities seriously and, more damagingly, to take seriously the words that were eventually chosen·*

*The lack of purpose meant, despite the cost, we produced little of any real value·*

The POST mnemonic might not always be the most appropriate, and many trainers prefer other methods of planning. You do, nevertheless, still need to have a focus on what you want your participants to learn.

You could use a *mind map* to sketch out what you need to cover. The node in the centre would be your overall purpose or focus. Each second-level node could then become an objective, which may in turn become the key point(s) for each session. You can draw further lines and nodes from these to help you work out what you need to include, and perhaps also the activities and resources you will require for each.

## PLANNING TEMPLATES

You will notice that we haven't provided a template for you to use. This is because you are responsible for working out what works for you using some or all of the ingredients above.

The ways in which we plan include:

- looking at what we need to cover and how much time we have, and setting out in a document a clear and logical sequence of activities;

- thinking of the participants' end goal and devising a long list of activities from which we can choose to reach this, depending on their knowledge and understanding;
- keeping in mind a 'golden thread' that sets the purpose and objectives of the training;
- using PowerPoint as a visual organiser.

*Imagine your training is like a stick of rock: when you break it in half, what does it say in the middle? These words are the core of your session.*

*When I was asked to deliver a training session on 'Mathematical Literacy' I needed to decide what my stick of rock would say. Clearly, mathematical literacy was my focus, but what was the essence of my training session going to be?*

*While I am passionate about mathematics, not everyone is, often because they perceive they are not very good at it. I had 60 minutes to convince the participants in my training session that they were all good at mathematics in order for them to value and acknowledge the importance of mathematical literacy.*

*The session included many elements that built up the participants' knowledge gradually (definitions, evidence from students, active learning tasks involving cloakroom tickets) but finally we paused on the importance of having positive dispositions towards mathematics in order to recognise and appreciate the importance of mathematical literacy everywhere.*

*So, what did my stick of rock say? I love maths. I love maths. I love maths.*

*This was my key message – to be over the top with how we talk about and view mathematics among the students and adults we engage with. By doing this, we will begin to see that mathematical literacy does indeed affect every single one of us and that we can all do it.*

# TIMING

Whenever you are training, you will have a fixed amount of time in which to meet your objectives. You need to plan accordingly, and confidently share the schedule with the participants at the beginning of your training event. You should make clear the start and finish times of each session in the day. And, to show you respect their time, you should always do your best to be ready when you say the participants should be.

It is sensible to agree a rule at the beginning about keeping to time. Hopefully this will mean that participants are not late to sessions, but what should you do if they are?

Most people will be apologetic and take their own responsibility for catching up. If the participants who were on time are already engaged in a task, you may want to have a quick chat with the latecomer to ensure they know what to do. If you have begun presenting some new information, do not feel the need to repeat all you have already said as this will be unfair on those who were there at the start. Instead, summarise when you have finished speaking so that the latecomer can pick up the key points, and follow up with them at a moment that is convenient to you.

If someone is persistently late, you may need to have a quiet word with them, particularly if they are affecting others' learning. Remember, of course, that your participants are adults and need to be treated accordingly.

It is important to keep as far as possible to the schedule you have set out, but do remember that (as we discussed in **Chapter 2**) everyone has a lot going on in their lives. There may be a vital reason for making a call at a fixed time, they may need to take medication or they wish to get some fresh air after being in a stuffy room. You will need time to catch your breath too.

Sometimes teachers, especially if they are attending training on what would otherwise be a normal school day, will suggest you shorten the day by missing breaks or abbreviating sessions they claim are less relevant to them. Before you agree to do this, consider your contract, if you have one, and also the needs of the whole group. At workshops we have led in certain parts of the world, some teachers have travelled long and far to be in our sessions. They want to make the most of every second, to gain every ounce of learning they can from the allotted time. We cannot overstate how important it is to be aware of such expectations and to meet them, regardless of the pressure from other participants.

As a trainer, time is both your friend and your enemy. With experience you will get to know how long an activity should take, which activities work best after others and which are more appropriate at certain times of the day. It is demanding, for example, to expect too much mental agility immediately before or after a lunch break. It can also be a good idea to get people physically moving first thing in the afternoon, even if just to swap groups.

A typical whole training day might look something like one of the following examples.

**Table 5.2**  Training day – four sessions of equal length

| | |
|---|---|
| Session 1 | 09.00 – 10.30 |
| Break | 10.30 – 11.00 |
| Session 2 | 11.00 – 12.30 |
| Lunch | 12.30 – 13.30 |

| Session 3 | 13.30 – 15.00 |
| Break | 15.00 – 15.30 |
| Session 4 | 15.30 – 17.00 |

**Table 5.3**  Training day – three sessions of unequal length

| Introduction | 09.00 – 09.30 |
| Session 1 | 09.30 – 11.00 |
| Break | 11.00 – 11.30 |
| Session 2 | 11.30 – 12.30 |
| Lunch | 12.30 – 13.30 |
| Session 3 | 13.30 – 15.30 |
| Conclusion | 15.30 – 16.00 |

**Table 5.4**  Training day – six sessions of equal length

| Session 1 | 09.00 – 10.00 |
| Session 2 | 10.00 – 11.00 |
| Break | 11.00 – 11.15 |
| Session 3 | 11.15 – 12.15 |
| Session 4 | 12.15 – 13.15 |
| Lunch | 13.15 – 14.00 |
| Session 5 | 14.00 – 15.00 |
| Break | 15.00 – 15.15 |
| Session 6 | 15.15 – 16.15 |

It can often be a good idea to have sessions of an equal length, as it helps everyone pace their day. Ninety minutes is probably the maximum period of concentration both for you and your participants – and by this we mean of course that these 90 minutes should contain a variety of activities. If you are regularly running out of time and tempted to go on for longer than this, you may need to review how much you are trying to cover in each session.

Try not to be either too rigid or overambitious with what you have planned to do. Otherwise, being a trainer will become a stressful experience and you may not end up meeting your objectives. Less is often more, but be sure to do it well. Be flexible enough as well to accommodate your participants' shifting needs.

Be ready with more material if you get ahead of time. This could, for example, be an impromptu but focused plenary discussion, a paper-based activity you have prepared, something you could write on the board or flipchart or, if you are using software such as PowerPoint or Keynote, some 'hidden' slides you can skip to. The trick is for participants to think that you have delivered everything on time and have prepared with precision!

And when the training session has finished, do not look like you are in a hurry to escape. Make yourself available at the end to answer questions and chat with participants, as many of them will value this, perhaps having been too shy to ask specific questions in front of other people. It is another opportunity as well to gauge whether you met their objectives.

# STRUCTURE

The way you plan your training *sessions* will of course be quite similar to how you would plan your lessons. Think carefully about how you will structure and scaffold learning. Plan how you will increase the complexity and depth of your topic.

Consider how you might differentiate the activities you ask participants to do, especially if you discover their prior knowledge is variable. Just as with differentiation with children, this can be through creating alternative tasks and outcomes, or providing different levels of support.

Make sure your training day overall, and each session within it, has coherence and is properly sequenced. When you are preparing, play your plan through in your mind and think of yourself as being a member of the audience. Does the order of activities make sense? Are there clear stages in the development of the participants' understanding? Think how one session could flow to the next, or how you might want to provide a natural break from one topic to the next.

You will normally need to go through several drafts of your plan before you feel it is right.

# TASKS

In the same way as you would aim to do with students, set your participants up for success in each task. Make sure they have understood what you have asked them to do, especially if you are going to be asking them for feedback in a plenary session after a specified period of time. Adults can be quite badly disciplined when working on a task in pairs or groups without direct supervision.

Some trainers like to write up their training plan with one column stating clearly what they will be doing or saying and another stating what the participants will be doing at the same time. If you are speaking, they are listening. If you are asking them to discuss the answer to a question in pairs, write in your column what you will say and in their column what they will do. This makes you think carefully about the instructions you will give.

When asking participants to do an activity, one approach is to follow a five-point rule (you should do this in the order you think is most suitable for your style and context).

1.  Describe the activity orally.
2.  Provide clear instructions on a slide or piece of paper.
3.  Demonstrate the activity either by gesture or showing an example.
4.  Ask someone among the participants to repeat what you have asked.
5.  Quickly check that each person, pair or group understands the task and is getting on with it as soon as you can after the allotted time has begun.

Sometimes you may want to give instructions which are less prescriptive. The participants will discover their own ways of working and completing the task. The discussions at the end of the activity can consequently be very rich and draw on both content and pedagogical technique.

Three types of activity you will need to control carefully are plenary discussions, the open sharing of ideas and question and answer sessions. For each of these, you may first need to set or agree some rules and be ready to referee what is being said or suggested.

More confident participants can dominate any of these types of activities. As a trainer, you need to be aware of this and encourage quieter participants to have their say if they want to. In a feedback session following a group activity, you might deliberately want to nominate a spokesperson for each table who is not someone whose voice has already been heard a lot. It is also important that you remain in control so that questions or points that are being made are channelled through you as the facilitator of the session.

You will also need to be wary not to set yourself up for failure. You may have planned the rest of the training very carefully, but the participants may catch you out when they are given a free voice! We will look more closely in **Chapter 8** at how to involve your audience.

## BEGINNINGS AND ENDINGS

Cognitive psychologists talk about the serial position effect, better known as primacy and recency. This refers to the tendency to remember the first and last items on a list better than those in the middle. We are often told as well to create a good impression, and a lasting one.

This has implications both for how you structure each part of your training sessions, and also how you introduce yourself at the beginning and say goodbye at the end. Let's start at the beginning, and look as well at how you might calm some initial nerves.

You may already have some of your own tried and tested methods for preparing to perform in front of a new group, but here are three basic steps you might take.

1. *Rehearse your opening.* You may have watched someone else and presumed it is easy to improvise, but you may not have been aware that this person has in fact thought hard about, and maybe even practised out loud, their first lines. Write down the key points so that you can refer to them if you need to. It is not always necessary to have the exact words, but it can be helpful to know what you intend to say. Your 'script' might begin with a comment about the weather or a joke at your own expense. But it would normally also set the tone for the session by stating clearly who you are and why you are there.
2. *Get in the zone.* If you watch an athlete about to run a race, you will see their focus. They will tune out distractions, they may have a routine, they will be playing ahead in their mind the start of the race and maybe even every section of it. Give yourself some time on your own before you start so that you feel ready to do what you have planned. Reread your script, rearrange your desk and materials, put your phone to one side. Take some deep breaths and channel any nerves positively into adrenalin.
3. *Show your human side.* Smile, appear welcoming, gain rapport with your audience. Your role is to train your participants, to transform their practice, but your job will be made

much easier if you take care not to set yourself apart. Let them know either that you were once in their position or that you can assimilate their questions and concerns. Demonstrate humility as well as confidence.

When I think about structure, I think about three things: What's the training about? What does my audience know already? And how do I build a relationship with my audience?

So, the first session of the day tries to account for all three. I use a few different formats but let's talk about one in particular. First, I give a brief introduction to the topic, and then I ask them questions about what they think and feel about the topic.

Depending on the answer required, participants with different responses have to line themselves up differently or go to different corners of the room. For example, I could ask 'How important is formative assessment?' If they think 'very', they go to one corner; if they think 'slightly', they go to a different corner. Or I can make the response required more 'continuous'. I could ask them 'How prevalent is formative assessment in your school?', and get them to line up in order, from 'very' to 'not at all'.

To do this, they need to talk to each other, to explore each other's ideas before deciding on their place in the line. Once they have reached their position, I interview them, receiving every answer positively – even if it displays a misunderstanding, I take that and use it in a positive way.

What does this format achieve? It starts the day well. Why? I get to talk to individuals, starting to build a relationship. They get to talk to each other, starting to build their relationships. I find out what they know. I allow those with lots to say to talk, but only briefly, and I actively encourage those who are shy. By the end of this opening session, they understand my purpose, they feel like they know me, I have a better appreciation of their starting points, and I know some names, which helps me keep those relationships going throughout the day.

And let's finish with the end, by which time you will hopefully be on good terms with your participants and you will all be sad to say your farewells. It is easy to run out of time to close properly, but you should try your best to do so. Ideally, you would have allowed space in the schedule for a summary of what you have covered, some action points to take away, and a reflection by the participants on what was most useful.

In **Chapter 3** we discussed how to help adults know what to take away, and in **Chapter 12** we will consider how to evaluate and reflect on yourself as a trainer. Your closing session gives you the opportunity to take the temperature on immediate reactions and reflections. It is an important moment as well to check that you have met your participants' expectations and your objectives. And it is also time to test if your training had purpose.

## TOOLKIT CHECKLIST

When planning your training course, you can now ask yourself the following questions.

- Have I understood the *why* and the *what* of my training sessions?
- Have I thought about how to make the best use of my time?
- Have I structured my sessions effectively?
- Have I opened and closed my training sessions with impact?

# 6

# MATERIALS

## KEY WORDS IN THIS CHAPTER

- materials
- resources
- needs
- venue

- flipchart
- white board
- digital tools

### IN THIS CHAPTER YOU WILL:

- think about the resources you will need in a training session;
- think about how to choose and design learning materials;
- reflect upon issues of intellectual property.

## RESOURCES

Let's imagine that you are training in a venue you've never visited before. You have your presentation and materials on a memory stick and you are assuming that there will be a laptop available. When you get there, there's no laptop! Disaster!

To avoid disaster, you need to think ahead. Use the checklist in Table 6.1 below to make sure you have got 'all the basics' covered.

**Table 6.1**    Checklist of basic resources to take with you or to request from the venue

| | Required? | How many? | Responsibility (Venue / Me) |
|---|---|---|---|
| Laptop | | | |
| Data projector | | | |
| Flipchart stand and flipchart paper | | | |
| Whiteboard | | | |
| Flipchart/whiteboard pens (preferably multi-coloured) | | | |
| Amplifier and speakers (if you require sound – a venue may often have a sound system of its own, but it's worth checking!) | | | |
| Extension lead | | | |
| DVD player (or DVD drive in laptop) | | | |
| Camera to take photographs during the session | | | |
| Copies of your presentation and materials (on USB, on the laptop and in your email/ cloud account just in case!) | | | |
| Paper copies of handouts/workbooks | | | |
| Blank A4 paper | | | |
| Blank A3 paper | | | |
| Sticky notes (preferably multi-coloured) | | | |
| Pens and pencils for participants | | | |
| Glue/sticky tape | | | |
| Multi-coloured paper and card | | | |
| Notebooks for participants to use | | | |
| White tack | | | |
| Name labels (including one for you!) | | | |
| Scissors | | | |
| Stopwatch (physical or for projection) | | | |
| Something to make a noise to catch participants' attention. | | | |

Think about how essential each item on the checklist could be. For example, if you know that sticky notes are essential, take them with you! And if you know that particular resources are important for all the training courses you do, put them in a box and take the box with you from training course to training course.

## TAKE A MOMENT

Don't be afraid to add items to the list in Table 6.1. For example, Alison likes taking along small pieces of card to hang on a washing line to display participants' ideas. Think about the extra items you would add to the list, and create your own version of Table 6.1.

In the final column of the checklist, there's a column headed 'Responsibility'. It is really important to decide whether *you* are going to bring particular resources with you or whether you are expecting the venue to supply them. If you expect the venue to supply them, ensure you find out who is responsible at the venue and send them your list (including any requests for the photocopying of materials!) in good time. Likewise, try to visit the venue well before the training (the night before, or early that morning) to ensure the materials and resources you are expecting have arrived.

Even if you've requested resources in advance, things can still go wrong. When undertaking a course abroad, I was collected from the hotel to visit the venue. It was a great space. I familiarised myself with the audio system, I loaded up my presentation onto the computer in the room, and I rearranged the seating to ensure things were ready for the morning. I even put out sticky notes ready for the first session.

It was only then that I realised my materials were missing: there were no sets of photocopies. I had ordered these several weeks before; I had even had a reply to confirm receipt. Luckily, my contact person was there with me. She realised there had been a mistake, she took an electronic copy of those materials which needed photocopying, and the following morning she arrived with everything done. I was really grateful to her. So what did I learn?

Never rely on resources or materials actually being where you expect them to be. Always take a copy of everything on a memory stick, in case you need to photocopy or buy materials or resources in an emergency! If it's really important – take it with you! Always have a back-up plan.

*These points were brought home to me on another occasion when travelling with a co-trainer, who was coordinating a multi-venue trip. He had the resources and materials in his bag, and as we entered a particular country it became clear he had an immigration problem. I continued my journey to the hotel (which was also the training venue), only to be woken at 6am the next morning by a phone call. My co-trainer had been deported because his passport was not valid for a full six months.*

*I leapt out of bed and immediately rewrote parts of the presentation, thinking about how to achieve the same objectives without resources and materials. Where it was impossible, I asked the hotel staff to step in and photocopy or acquire what I needed. Luckily, I had the resources and materials for the first session in my own bag, and I had my handouts on a USB stick, so the hotel had some time to get everything ready for the rest of the day.*

*In short, be ready to adapt and pre-empt problems as much as you can.*

When you are at the venue, checking through resources and materials, make sure you put them where they need to be – it will make your training course run more smoothly. If every table needs A4 paper throughout the course, put it on the tables straightaway. Likewise, if you need particular sets of resources or materials for particular parts of the training, group them together so it's easy for you to find them and distribute them efficiently at the correct time.

*Imagine the worst-case scenario. You have not been able to get to the venue early; when you do get there, you realise the resources are missing and you have five minutes to improvise. The only thing you can do is to look around the training room (or even just outside the door) for inspiration.*

*In one training course where I ask participants to make models, I usually request paper, card, scissors and other similar resources.*

*(Continued)*

*(Continued)*

*On two occasions they weren't there. On one of those occasions, I found newspapers outside the door and asked participants to make models out of them. On another, I used the boxes which some photocopied materials had arrived in and some plastic cups from a drinks dispenser.*

*In fact, an empty box can be useful in all sorts of ways: you can use it to collect participants' answers, you can open out the box to a flat surface for groups to present their ideas on, or individual participants can use pieces of a box as a mini-whiteboard to show you their ideas.*

*Indeed, using resources in novel or unexpected ways can create a huge impact. If you want to divide your audience into groups, try putting different coloured stickers under their chair before the training starts. When you ask them to rearrange themselves into different coloured groups, they love the surprise and any resentment they may have felt in having to move is quickly forgotten. Likewise, on one occasion when the microphone didn't work, I rolled up a piece of paper and wrote 'microphone' on it. To my surprise, the audience responded very positively, finding it funny but also respecting the fact that the person holding the microphone should be listened to.*

# MATERIALS

Learning materials include things like Microsoft PowerPoint or Apple Keynote presentations, handouts, workbooks, card-based activities, posters, videos and visual aids.

Think about the aims of your training course – perhaps you want participants to learn about effective group work. You should therefore choose materials which will help you achieve your aims. For example, a video of effective group work is likely to be important. A worksheet of questions about the video may be even more effective.

So, when thinking about materials, consider:

- what participants will do;
- what participants will think about while they are doing it;
- what participants will learn.

And then design or choose your materials to make those three things happen. For example:

- materials can provide procedural information (telling participants what to do) or factual information through a handout, video or PowerPoint;

- a handout with an image and a set of questions about the image may be designed to make participants think in order to learn.

Usually, it's best to design materials yourself, as the aims for your course are likely to be different to the aims of other trainers and training courses. However, if appropriate, seek inspiration from materials on the internet. But don't blindly download and employ them – it will just end in disaster.

Sometimes, an organisation may provide you with materials. While the materials will have been quality-assured, they may not absolutely fit the context in which you are training. You should check with the organisation about how flexible you can be. Most organisations would allow you to adapt the materials, providing you still meet their objectives. If in doubt, ask!

# DESIGNING MATERIALS EFFECTIVELY

So, now we've thought about the purpose of materials, it's important to think about different types of learning material in turn and how to design and employ them successfully.

# PRESENTATIONS

Filling slides full of information and reading it aloud does not help your participants to learn and can easily put them to sleep. As soon as some participants see a presentation, they switch off. Even if you are trying to explain the ideas on a slide, your participants cannot read the slide and listen to you. And while you are reading it, you may end up with your back to the audience, so your participants feel less engaged.

However, presentations are useful for providing structure to your session. You may have a slide to introduce each different section, to provide basic information, to give procedural instructions (for example, about an activity), to emphasise key points or to prompt thinking and discussion. Try to stick to our design checklist in Table 6.2.

**Table 6.2**  Design checklist for presentation slides

| Have I . . . ? | ✓ or ✗ |
|---|---|
| 1. chosen a simple design template for my slides? | |
| *You may have to use the design template provided by the organisation.* | |
| 2. used consistent fonts, avoided capital letters and avoided too many different styles (like **bold**, *italic* and <u>underline</u>) and special effects? | |
| *Although it's tempting to use a range of fonts and styles and to use capital letters throughout, they make the slide harder to read. Special effects, such as animations and transitions, can be distracting.* | |

*(Continued)*

**Table 6.2**   (Continued)

| Have I . . . ? | ✓ or ✗ |
| --- | --- |

3.  used a pale, non-white background (it reduces glare) and dark text for good contrast?

    *This is not only important for reading, but some participants may use a translation app, and so good contrast is essential for the app to recognise your text. Avoid red and green, just in case you have colour blind people in the room.*

4.  put the main messages on the screen rather than all the details?

    *Even just putting a question on a slide can prompt your explanation and participants' thinking.*

5.  embedded a graph, figure, animation, simulation or video into a slide, instead of lots of words?

    *Not using words may communicate the key ideas more effectively and prompt your explanation more effectively. If you are using images, make sure they are sharp and relevant and that you acknowledge their source, especially if they are copyrighted.*

6.  written out the instructions for an activity in detail?

    *Display the instructions throughout the activity, just in case your participants forget what they are supposed to be doing or discussing.*

The only time when it may be useful to include more words on a presentation slide is when working with participants who have English as an additional language. If you summarise your explanation on a slide, then your participants have a little more time to translate. ·

Finally, here are four very pragmatic tips to avoid unexpected problems.

1.  Don't forget to check your slides before the training course starts, particularly if you're using them on someone else's laptop. Even on your own computer, they may still look different when projected.
2.  If you have a remote control or remote mouse, make sure it works and that you know how to use it. You usually have to plug in a USB dongle before the session. Always take spare batteries.
3.  Make sure you know what buttons to press if no image appears on the projector screen. This depends on your computer, but you should be able make the image appear on the computer screen and on the projector.
4.  If you find your audience are staring at the screen and not listening to you, blank the screen. On PowerPoint, you can do so by pressing B!

## TAKE A MOMENT

Find a presentation you have used before in teaching or in training. Evaluate it based on the points above. What are its strengths and weaknesses, and how would you improve it? Think about the purpose and design of each slide.

*If participants are expecting information delivery, they often expect a copy of your slides when they walk into the room, with space alongside each slide to make notes. Indeed, many training venues make a copy of your presentation 'by default' and put it into participants' 'delegate packs'.*

*I always remove the presentation from their packs. Why?*

- *Because I want to build up the ideas as the day progresses. I tend to have discussion activities to make participants think before using the presentation to collate their ideas and summarise key points. If they see these key points before doing the activities, the activities don't work effectively and participants don't engage in thinking.*
- *Participants can pre-judge the training before it happens. If they look at the slides and think they know it all, they can disengage. But in fact, much of the learning comes from the discussions they have rather than just from the ideas being delivered.*

## EFFECTIVE USE OF PAPER MATERIALS

Some participants feel like they haven't been to a training course without some paper 'take-away' materials. However, any paper materials should help participants to think and talk about what you want them to learn rather than just provide information.

They may include instructions, information or pro formas to record their thinking. They could include handouts, question sheets, blank mind maps, posters, A5 cards, card-sorts, etc.

You can see our advice for paper materials below. Do try to minimise the paper materials you use. This is good for the planet, and the less dependent you are on photocopied materials the more resilient you are when things go wrong! Try to recycle any spare materials.

'If you want a small group to work together on a handout, photocopy it on A3 paper rather than just on A4.'

'Keep it simple. Just like with presentations, don't use capital letters, lots of different fonts, or too many different styles (such as bold, italics or underscoring).'

'Keep the text well spaced out. You want to make it easy to read.'

'Don't give out materials when you are talking. Your audience cannot do two things at once. They are either listening to you or looking at the materials.'

'If you want to explain what to do with a handout or activity, project a copy on the screen and talk it through.'

'If you are using a lot of handouts, consider stapling them together into a workbook to avoid chaos on participants' desks.'

'If some materials are finished with, tidy them up before giving out others. It helps your participants to focus.'

'Don't expect participants to engage with information-heavy handouts during the session. If you must have them, give them out at the end.'

'Give out any lists of further reading on paper. If you put them on a presentation, your participants will not have time to write them down.'

## EFFECTIVE USE OF FLIPCHARTS AND WHITEBOARDS

Flipcharts, whiteboards and marker pens? You may think they are old-fashioned, but they are still some of the most valuable tools you have. So, why use a flipchart or whiteboard?

They are the easiest way to record your participants' ideas. This values their ideas and helps to promote their engagement in discussion. It also demonstrates to them that the training is relevant to them. You can write their ideas down or ask them to record ideas on a sticky note and then rearrange the ideas on the flipchart.

They provide an easy place to build up a sequence of ideas or to put structure on ideas. Thinking about the way in which ideas relate together and building them up graphically with words, arrows and flow charts (often in response to participants' contributions) can really help your participants to follow what you are saying.

If you have enough flipcharts or simply large sheets of paper, you can give participants ownership of their learning by asking them to discuss a topic in small groups and record their thinking to present to the whole group.

Using a whiteboard or flipchart suggests to your participants that the training is 'for them'. It's not just the same presentation you've rolled out before.

So, what do you need to think about when using flipcharts?

1. Take markers with you. (If you are using a whiteboard, make sure you only use 'dry-wipe' markers on it – and don't use any markers at all on an interactive whiteboard!)
2. Make sure the flipchart is positioned high up on its stand so everyone can see it.
3. Check if the paper is too thin or shiny. If so, the marker won't write on it properly and the writing from one side of the paper may show through to the other.
4. If you expect to draw something complicated on a flipchart, outline it in pencil first before the session.

## EFFECTIVE USE OF DIGITAL TOOLS

If you are training in a school, the room may have an interactive whiteboard. To exploit the interactivity, you usually need to use the computer which is already there, so take your presentation on a USB memory stick.

Apart from presentations, the whiteboard gives you touch-access to a multitude of resources on the internet, including videos, simulations, animations, podcasts, etc. The benefits of using digital tools include:

- linking the workshop to everyday contexts;
- improving engagement and motivation;
- supporting exploration, experimentation, collaboration and discussion;
- focusing attention on particular concepts, helping to challenge misconceptions.

Asking participants to use their phones or tablets can also open up other opportunities for learning.

- Kahoot or Quizlet are online quiz tools which help you and your participants to assess their learning and survey their ideas.
- Padlet enables participants to place virtual sticky notes on a wall. If they work in groups, you can then display and rearrange all the sticky notes from each group together to build up ideas and conclusions.
- Slack is a team collaboration tool, where participants can work together on a task, even if they are not sitting next to each other.
- WhatsApp allows participants to communicate if they have a task which takes different members of the same group to different locations.
- Poll Everywhere is an audience response tool which you can use for quick surveys of your participants.

**TAKE A MOMENT**

Familiarise yourself with each of the apps above. What are the advantages and disadvantages of each in helping participants to think together?

If you intend to use any app during the training, ensure you have notified participants that they will need a mobile phone or a tablet, and check that your app works on both Android and Apple platforms. Check also that the app or website works in whichever country you are training in. For example, Google applications do not work in China.

# INTELLECTUAL PROPERTY

Imagine you have found a handout or worksheet which has been designed by someone else, and does not quite fit your purpose. However, it may have inspired you to design your own, or you may want to use particular sections from it. For example, you may like some of the questions on a handout or you may want to use a short section of video from a longer sequence.

Although teachers often do this for their school classes, when training adults in particular make sure you are not infringing someone else's intellectual property, particularly if you are being paid to deliver training. At the start of any DVD, there is a notice which licenses that DVD for individual use but prohibits you playing it to an audience. Of course, some companies produce training materials for you to purchase and use 'at will'. However, if you use those resources without purchasing them, you are in breach of the company's intellectual property rights.

For education, rights holders will sometimes be accommodating. However, if you make a profit from someone else's intellectual property, they may be justified in asking for a share of your profit! Also, different countries have different copyright rules (in the UK, copyright is governed by the Intellectual Property Office – part of the government), so if you want to use a passage from a book make sure you have checked the copyright rules in your country. At the very least, always credit the owner/creator of particular materials. This is also true of images. Do not assume that because you have found something on the internet you can use it without saying where it came from. At the very least, you should display the URL in small text on the slide itself.

You can find out more about materials which have been shared for reuse at **www.creativecommons.org**. You can even search for resources which have been shared with different licences for commercial and non-commercial reuse.

## TAKE A MOMENT

Imagine you want to use a photocopy of a published book as part of your training. Find out the rules in your country which govern how much of that book you can photocopy and how many times you can photocopy it.

## TOOLKIT CHECKLIST

When planning your training course, you can now ask yourself the following questions.

- Have I made a list of the basic resources I will need in a training session?
- Have I learnt how to choose and design learning materials effectively?
- Have I understood the importance of intellectual property?

# 7
# ENVIRONMENT

## KEY WORDS IN THIS CHAPTER

- environment
- space
- location

- furniture
- accessories
- welcoming

### IN THIS CHAPTER YOU WILL:

- think about participants' first impressions of the training environment;
- consider how to organise your furniture to suit the training requirements;
- decide if you need to accessorise the room with your own props;
- understand the different purposes a training environment can serve.

The way you set up your training environment can both entice and relax your audience. It can be an extension of your own character and personality. You should try to 'own' it as much as possible.

Wherever possible, try to find out in advance as much as you can about where you will be training.

Here is a list of what you may want to know prior to your session:

- space – is it a room? corridor? lecture theatre? how big/small? shape? size? location?
- chairs – adult friendly? separate or attached to tables?
- tables – how many? what size? shape?

- flipchart/s and pens – provided?
- a table at the front for your equipment – provided?
- wall space – able to stick/pin paper to?
- stationery – will there be paper, pens, sticky notes, white tack, wall pins provided?
- do you need to bring your own laptop? will there be internet? will there be a projector?
- function – is the environment designed to be a training facility or is it simply a space for you to train in?

This last point is particularly important as it will provide a frame of reference for you to consider in the lead up to the training. Specifically appointed training environments should offer a basic provision of requirements compared to a makeshift space.

Of course, you may not be able to learn anything about your training space before you arrive. Even if you do, there is always the chance that it can change too! So, it is worth planning ahead for any eventuality. For example, you may have included activities that require participants to sit around tables (for example, a card sort or the design of a poster). Equally, if your training session uses role play, you may not require much furniture yet be faced with a room full of it. So, when confronted with the unexpected, adapt quickly, smoothly and if possible without your participants knowing! This may sound difficult, but if something you planned is impossible, just think why you had decided to do it and then think quickly about how to achieve the same ends.

# FIRST IMPRESSIONS

When participants enter the training environment, you might want them to be surprised, amazed or curious, but above all you want to put them at ease. You can achieve this in several ways.

Firstly, consider what participants might expect to see or not see. Put yourself in their shoes and view the environment through their eyes. Does it look friendly? professional? enticing? scary? What might they be expecting? Does the environment reflect the training content? For example, if the training session is subject specific, does the environment mirror this?

Secondly, the environment may also be as unfamiliar to your participants as it is to you. In some ways this is easier to manage, as nobody has any preconceived ideas about the layout or expectations of how the session will run.

On the other hand, participants may be extremely familiar with the environment (it could even be a classroom they have been teaching in all day or a staff room they view as a relaxing 'off work' zone). While this is potentially more challenging, it is still important to make a good first impression, perhaps by changing the layout slightly or including an unusual object or item.

However much baggage (see **Chapter 2**) participants may arrive with, if your training environment looks active, enticing and inviting, they are more likely to leave that baggage behind.

**TAKE A MOMENT**

Think about a situation you have been faced with recently: for example, going for an interview, meeting new friends, etc. Now consider how the environment either helped or hindered you. Did the space help to calm nerves or add to them? Did it give you a sense of what was to follow? How did it impact on your overall first impressions of the situation?

# FURNITURE

One question for you to consider is should you move the furniture? Often the training environment will be a multi-functional space, used for many different training sessions. On the other hand, it may be a space familiar to you and your participants (for example, a classroom in your school). In either situation, you need to 'own' the space and participants need to regard the environment as a place of training.

So, if at all possible, we always advise moving even a little of the furniture. This helps you to stamp your own mark. It immediately gives you a sense of control. Always ask yourself: is the room/space fit for purpose or could it be enhanced a little?

*Sometimes when I find myself in a room that is impossible to rearrange due to the space and the layout of the tables and chairs, I will move the flipchart from one side of the room to the other. Does this in any way make a difference? No – but it means I have imprinted a little on the room!*

However, it is rare that the environment will be set up according to your specific requirements. When tables have been set into rows, you have planned group work; when only chairs are provided you had envisaged a horseshoe of tables. You get the idea!

While time-consuming, it is really important to ensure you can deliver the training session in the way you have planned. Don't be afraid to ask for tables and chairs to be added or taken away. And if you do rearrange (particularly if it is a colleague's classroom), remember to return it to its original format after you have finished. A top tip here is to take a photograph before you begin rearranging as it can save a lot of time trying to recall the original set up at the end!

Once you have decided upon the arrangement of tables and chairs, look around at the other furniture you have. For example, is there a table for your resources (if you need one)? Have flipcharts been provided? Are the screen and projector (if you are using them) where you want them?

You may be limited by how much you can change. However, just thinking through the possible options is a start and will still give you a sense of ownership. Remember, the space can really help to set the stage for the training to follow.

# ACCESSORIES

We all have different training styles. Some trainers love to use accessories or props, others prefer to let the content 'do the talking'. However, you need to be as comfortable as possible when training and if using a few props enables you to do this, then go for it!

Props can come in all shapes and sizes. For some trainers, having a few sticky notes available is sufficient, but for others certain accessories help them to accentuate the training content and 'bring it to life'. It is useful to think about props in two categories.

First, there are stationery props, such as:

- paper;
- pens;
- flipchart markers;
- different coloured marker pens;
- different types of paper (size: A4, A3, flipchart; colour: white or coloured; type: plain, lined, dotty);
- sticky notes (different colours, shapes and sizes);
- white tack or wall pins (to display participants' work with);
- scissors;
- glue;
- paper clips;
- highlighters.

Second, there are props that fit with training sessions, such as:

- puppets (e.g. to stimulate debates, to take the focus away from the participants, to support creativity and imagination);
- washing line and pegs (e.g. for displaying ideas, objectives or vocabulary);
- mystery bags (e.g. to hide resources, create an element of surprise, encourage collaboration);
- subject-specific props (e.g. dice for mathematics, magnets for science, fiction books for English).

It is amazing how you can set participants' expectations simply from a few coloured pens on a table! However, it is not so much the pens, but what they stand for. Different coloured pens on a table do not suggest that a test or exam is imminent, for example. They symbolise possible collaboration between colleagues, perhaps as a result of some thinking and reflecting. Of course, none of this may be true, but it serves to help, not hinder, the training session to follow.

With any of our training tips it is important to use props that you are comfortable with. One of our colleagues is amazing at using origami in her sessions, but this is not our forte (yet) and so we would appear less confident and participants would be able to tell!

*I have recently discovered extra-large, neon-coloured sticky notes. I have been using them in most training sessions I have been running and I am yet to run a session where at least one participant fails to comment on them in some excited way!*

*A simple but very pleasing and cost-effective resource!*

## ENHANCING THE ENVIRONMENT

Once you are in full flow don't forget about the space you are in. Just as first impressions can make a difference, so can the use of the environment throughout the training. Whether you have one hour or five days, make the environment work for you. Any environment can be used for several different purposes.

For example, you may choose to ask participants to record ideas on a piece of flipchart paper so that you can then display this around the room. This works particularly well if you have an extended training session (perhaps over a day or two) as you can begin to create a working wall. This allows participants to reflect on what they thought and said and even allows them to begin to notice and possibly alter their viewpoints as the training progresses.

Equally, using the wall space is a good reminder of the quantity and value of the work participants have completed. If you are within a school environment often some of these pieces of paper can last after the event and serve as further discussion points for participants. We have sat in staff rooms where we can see a visible record of staff training on the walls.

Washing lines are another useful prop to enhance the environment. They can be used to display images you want participants to see and refer to, or they can be used to peg up and celebrate work from your participants. We often forget to celebrate the work of adults, but we all do respond well to a little praise now and then. If participants know the work will be pegged up, it tends to help focus their minds on doing a good job too!

You may have set a healthy competition between groups of participants. Displaying work from each group allows everyone to see how different groups have approached a task, and allows individuals to consider how they would repeat the task next time.

## ADAPTING THE ENVIRONMENT

If possible, it is useful – and fun – to adapt the environment so that it mirrors the context of the training session. Here are a few examples from training sessions we have run where we have been able to change the environment.

## EXAMPLE A – TRAINING IN THE STYLE OF A CAFE

Think about what a café environment conjures up. For example, the tables might have check tablecloths on them, there may be flowers or a candle (battery-operated, not real!) on the table, and there will be a range of hot drinks and almost certainly good quality biscuits or cakes. In addition, there is probably some ambient music playing in the background and the atmosphere is relaxed. Adapting the environment in such a dramatic way is particularly effective for different audiences you may be training. We have run Maths Cafés with groups of parents/carers who might not otherwise have wanted to attend a maths training session in school. Advertising it as a café and then adapting the environment appropriately has always worked extremely well. It helps to set the scene, relax the participants and disarm any potential anxiety people may have.

### TAKE A MOMENT

Think about a training session where you could adapt the environment so that it mirrors the context or content of the training.

## EXAMPLE B – MAKING A TOPIC MORE EXCITING

Make potentially boring training sessions more exciting by ambushing your participants with something unexpected! They may be assuming there will be lots of worksheets and limited activities, but this does not mean you have to meet their expectations. Why not surprise them by setting up a fun, colourful, exciting environment which offers a taste of the session to follow? You could achieve this by putting out large pieces of paper and coloured pens on each table, perhaps some unusual objects (e.g. a tennis ball, a packet of seeds) that you are going to use later on in the session or even sticking up some posters or photographs. Whatever it is, ask yourself: 'Will participants expect to see the tables or environment used in this way?'

## EXAMPLE C – USING SPACE WELL

When we run workshops to train teachers to be trainers, one of the activities we often do is a speed-sharing task (see Activity 38 in **Chapter 10**), where each participant has one minute to share an idea they have for a 15-minute presentation the following day with every other participant. In order to facilitate this activity, we need to adapt the environment. Two rows of chairs facing each other are required. On one occasion we were lucky enough to have a spare classroom in which we were able to adapt the environment without the participants seeing. On another occasion we created the two rows of chairs during a break, so that at least when participants came back the room was ready. This is a very simple yet effective way to make the environment work for you and your training needs.

## EXAMPLE D – TRAINING WITH A LARGE GROUP IN A LARGE SPACE

A particular session one of us ran had multiple challenges. The topic was huge, the time was limited (45 minutes) and the audience was large. This presents a different type of challenge with the environment needed to accommodate the audience. Firstly, if you are presenting in an auditorium the environment will be fixed in its layout of chairs in rows (no space for any tables). Secondly, any props you might use become redundant due to the sheer number of participants in attendance. However, knowing this in advance will allow you to prepare. In this case the participants can be your props! You can plan activities which involve them standing up to engage in tasks, so altering their perspective of the environment. You can also include actions where they have to vote with one, two or no hands in the air.

We hope that including these different training scenarios has shown you that anything is possible with the environment!

## CONSIDERING THE ENVIRONMENT

As with any decisions we make as trainers, we need to be socially and culturally sensitive.
Here are a few areas to consider:

- before moving any furniture check that this is acceptable – you may be in a country where men and women would not feel comfortable working together;
- if using stationery (such as pens, sticky notes, paper) make sure that these resources are available in the country where you are training;

- something as simple as playing music may not be acceptable; and finally . . .
- be prepared to lose a few resources! Occasionally participants accidentally pack away the odd pen or pack of sticky notes into their bags.

## TOOLKIT CHECKLIST

When planning your training course, you can now ask yourself the following questions.

- Have I found out about the environment ahead of the training session?
- Have I thought about the most appropriate arrangement of the furniture?
- Have I decided which props I would like to use?
- Have I viewed the training environment as an extension of my own character and personality?

# 8

# PRESENTATION

## KEY WORDS IN THIS CHAPTER

- presentation
- first impressions
- behaviour
- clothing

- eye contact
- ground rules
- language

### IN THIS CHAPTER YOU WILL:

- think about first impressions;
- consider how to be inclusive;
- explore your range of communication skills;
- review how to use presentation software.

People have often said that being in front of a group of children or adults is like being on stage. Having explored in the previous chapters how to prepare and make the most of the environment in which we are training, and how to select the best resources and materials to use, we are now going to look at how to put on a performance: what should you wear, how should you use your voice and gestures, how should you interact with the audience, and how might you ensure everyone has an enjoyable learning experience?

# FIRST IMPRESSIONS

It can take less than five seconds to form an opinion of somebody. This is not to say that initial impressions cannot be undone, but it does suggest that it is important to think carefully about how you want to look and act when the participants in your training session see you for the first time.

This underlines the importance of being ready and being early. If you rush in at the last minute looking flustered, spilling items from your bag, panicking about whether the technology will work, slopping coffee on the table or mumbling your opening words of introduction, it does not set a good tone for what will follow.

Let's rewind to the preparation stage and think of the essentials.

Firstly, how do you decide what to *wear*? If you are training in your own country or in an environment that is familiar, you should know what is culturally acceptable. If not, you will need to do some research.

Are the participants in your training group likely to be dressed smartly? If so, you should try to match this, partly out of respect for the effort they have made. Are the people in front of you likely to be sensitive about how much of your body is covered? If you are a man, should you wear a long-sleeved shirt? If you are a woman, can you show your shoulders and, if you are wearing a dress or skirt, how long should it be? Might you delight your audience if you wear something you have bought locally, such as a shalwar kameez or batik shirt?

Whatever you decide to wear, it is a good idea to remember two things: (a) make sure it is comfortable, especially when you are choosing your shoes as you will be on your feet a lot; and (b) consider that it is easier to start smart and become more casual as the day progresses (rather than the reverse). A good tip is to arrive in a jacket that you can then remove.

Some trainers have their own training outfit or something that accentuates their personality. Some ignore the suggestions above and wear clothes that make them look more approachable and allow them to kneel on the floor or jump around. These trainers are usually more experienced and focus more on substance than style. Wherever you fit on this spectrum, make 'how you look' a considered choice.

There are two things I think about when choosing my clothes.

First, do I need status with my audience? For example, a school teacher will usually dress smartly, wearing a jacket and/or a tie. They do this, not just because it is convention in the school, but also because they want to

(Continued)

*(Continued)*

*define their status, so the students will realise that they have to follow the teacher's instructions. Likewise, I dress smartly for an audience who are very senior, when I feel I need to communicate status very quickly. If I am working with officials from a Ministry of Education, for example, I will wear a jacket and tie. They have to believe in me, and by dressing smartly I am conveying the idea that I am a 'serious person' with 'value'.*

*On the other hand, sometimes you have to build a relationship very quickly with your audience and so 'dressing down' can help. This doesn't mean wearing ripped jeans! I wear 'smart-casual' because it gives the impression that I am not 'above' my audience but working alongside them as a peer. If you are training teachers, this is often a good approach, because they see you and your training as more authentic. They have to believe that you can teach, that you have worked in a classroom and that therefore what you say is important.*

*But if you're feeling nervous, dress as smartly as you like – it will give you confidence!*

Secondly, think about your *behaviour*. If some participants are already in your training room when you arrive, make eye contact and greet them at the earliest opportunity. If appropriate – again, be culturally aware here – shake their hands, welcome them, put them at ease. Walk tall and with purpose to the place where you are going to present. Begin to 'own' the environment by adjusting furniture and making it clear the stage is yours.

If, as is preferable, you are first in the room, try to let the participants enter only when you are ready for them. You may need to distribute some materials on tables, write something on the board, stick posters on walls, open the first slide of your presentation. If you have the luxury of preparing your room before anyone else sees it, use the time wisely so that the feel and look of the training is clear when the first people come into the room.

In practice, it can be difficult to keep people outside the room while you get everything ready. It can help break the ice if some of your participants help you distribute some of your resources or if you are chatting with them as you do so. You do need, however, to work out fast what should be where, even if you have not fully visualised it beforehand, and there must come a point where you decide the stage is set and you are ready to begin.

## GROUND RULES

You can create better conditions for learning if you decide with your group what the rules should be for the training room. These do not have to be lengthy or onerous but should be shared so that the participants can regulate each other's behaviour.

**TAKE A MOMENT**

What behaviour, both good and bad, have you noticed in other participants at training sessions you have attended? What are you like as a participant? Do you tend to do anything that might be considered particularly annoying or helpful? Be honest!

Here are some ideas to consider.

- Should mobile phones be set to silent?
- Should calls be taken outside the room (in some countries this is not expected)?
- Should everyone remain in the same seats for the whole training session?
- How will people listen to and respect each other's questions and opinions?
- How will everyone be given an opportunity to participate so that nobody dominates?

Most of the above can usually be managed implicitly, but you may feel safer making some of them clear at the start.

Perhaps the most important consideration is the last point. It is quite common to have one or two dominant participants and you need to be able to manage this so the rest of the group feels included. Think of ways to encourage quieter participants to ask or answer questions, give the dominant people specific roles in any group work and redistribute participants to different groups or tables at appropriate moments.

## BEING INCLUSIVE

It is still only relatively recently that neurodiversity has been recognised and celebrated. Neurodiversity refers to the acceptance that people can behave, react and think differently. Some people may have visible conditions; many others will have a hidden challenge or impairment that may affect their performance or interactions with others. We need to be mindful and respectful of other people's ways of being and the support they may require.

Table 8.1 contains a list of ten common areas you may come across at different levels.

**Table 8.1**  Common areas of neurodiversity

| | |
|---|---|
| Communication | Difficulties in speaking, listening, understanding |
| Concentration | Problems with attention, concentration, focus, impulsivity |
| Executive functions | Challenges with time management, organisation, reflection |
| Hearing | Congenital or acquired problems, in one or both ears |
| Literacy | Difficulties with reading, spelling, writing |

*(Continued)*

**Table 8.1**    (Continued)

| | |
|---|---|
| Mental/emotional | Depression, anxiety, eating disorders |
| Motor | Problems with coordination and balance |
| Numeracy | Challenges with maths-based activities |
| Physical | Congenital or acquired, visible or hidden problems |
| Visual | An impairment that can affect performance even with correction |

The list will be familiar to you if you are a teacher, and you may already know ways of identifying and making appropriate arrangements to include people who 'present' in these ways. It is sensible, for example, for those who are visually impaired to have a clear view of whatever you are presenting, and for those who have difficulty hearing to be somewhere acoustically appropriate, often near the front.

Most adults will have worked out how to deal with whatever specific challenges they have. As a trainer, just keep in mind that someone's behaviour may have explanations that are nothing to do with your training course. Simply focus on the positive, and if some people don't want to participate or appear uninterested, realise it may simply be neurodiversity in action.

# LANGUAGE USE

A major barrier to learning, especially in an international environment, can be communication. We have regularly led training sessions in English or French when it is not the first or even second language of any of the participants. Occasionally we have delivered training through an interpreter, which brings its own challenges – above all because of the unnatural distance it creates between you and the group.

Just because people can say hello, describe themselves and ask questions, it does not mean they are fluent in a language. The vocabulary is simple, and they will have used similar phrases many times. Linguists refer to this as basic interpersonal communication skills or social language.

More complex language, such as jargon or academic terms, can be much more challenging. Understanding instructions, reading lengthy texts and participating in discussions can be very difficult, stressful and off-putting. The same is true even for native speakers of the language if participants have not previously come across terminology or you have made wrong assumptions about their prior learning.

Here are five tips for supporting participants with the language demands of your training sessions.

1. *Plan what you want to say.* It is a good idea to script questions, instructions and explanations so that they are clear and meaningful. Read out loud to yourself what you have written down and revise it to make your language correct and succinct.
2. *Provide support.* Highlight key words and check understanding before asking your participants to use the language actively. Encourage them to ask if they do not understand what you are saying.

3.  *Use visuals and gestures.* If you are describing an activity you want your participants to do, show them or use images to assist your explanation. Perform an example of the activity, even in simple terms, such as holding up the resources they need to use.
4.  *Provide enough time.* It may take longer than expected for participants to do activities, especially if they have to read, write or express themselves. Also, give yourself enough time to speak at an appropriate pace to aid understanding.
5.  *Create a suitable environment.* Sometimes there is little you can do to change the layout of the room. Be aware, however, of distracting sounds. It may be helpful, for example, to turn off noisy ceiling fans or air-conditioning units while you are presenting, providing the room does not get too warm.

Likewise, if you want everyone in the room to learn from what is being said, you need to make sure they can hear it. If you are standing at the front of the room and someone in the first row is speaking, it is quite possible that those at the back will not hear. You can repeat what the person was saying, but it is better to get everyone into the habit of considering the needs of the rest of the group.

A simple way to train people to project their voice is to walk away from them (politely!) while they are speaking. They will want you to hear, so if you go to the far side of the room, they will speak much more loudly. As you may also know from being a teacher, a simple way to make everyone pay attention is to stand behind those who lack focus or who are chatting.

You should be conscious too of *non-verbal communication*. This refers to communication that is unwritten and unspoken, both intentional and unintentional. The main forms of non-verbal communication are facial expressions, body movement, gestures, eye contact, voice and touch. For example, your body language can inspire trust, but it can also offend, confuse or undermine what you are trying to convey. The way you stand, where you stand, how fast or how loudly you talk and whether you are prepared to sit with participants at their tables all send strong messages.

Even when you are silent, you are communicating non-verbally. If you should be listening to someone's contribution, are you focusing on them? Would it be useful to take notes? If the participants are working on an activity you have asked them to do, where will you be? You need to remain engaged. Again, move with purpose, interact with groups but give them space to learn on their own or together as well – only interrupt when you perceive it will be beneficial.

## USING PRESENTATION SLIDES

In **Chapter 6** we talked about the merits of using slides to aid your participants' understanding and present ideas, information and images. The quality of your slides and how you use them can say a lot about you as a trainer. Some people become over-reliant on them; others forget what they are projecting onto the screen and the slides can become distracting.

Your slides are another part of your theatrical performance. Done properly, a slide can provide focus, support those with language difficulties and create surprise. Microsoft PowerPoint or Apple Keynote provide a linear presentation; you may also be familiar with Prezi, which requires a lot of planning and can be used as a means of making a presentation appear more holistic.

There are many guides available that describe how best to use presentation software. Here are six tips that have worked for us.

1.  Know your slides, even if you did not design them yourself – print out a copy so that you can see what is coming up, and rehearse before you present.
2.  Do not read from your slides – they are for the audience, not the presenter, and be careful not to speak at them either or you will have your back to the audience.
3.  Learn how not to use your slides in a linear fashion – there are ways of skipping slides and going back, and you need to know how to do this both on a computer and, as far as is possible, using a remote clicker.
4.  Run your presentation from the desktop of the computer that is connected to the projector – if you run it from a memory stick plugged into the computer it can slow it down or it may stop working.
5.  Limit how many slides you use, in the same way that you should limit the amount of 'trainer talk' – if someone observes you train, ask them to note how much and how usefully you use the slides.
6.  Think outside the slide – the other materials you use, including both yourself and your interactions with your participants, as well as other visuals, whiteboards and flipcharts, should be strong enough to mean that you do not need to rely on what is on the screen.

## PUT YOURSELF IN THE AUDIENCE

All good performers try to imagine themselves from their audience's perspective. Remember that a main purpose of being a trainer is to transform other people's learning and understanding. If you present yourself and your materials in the right way, you will be an aid rather than a distraction. Substance and style go hand in hand and, as you become more experienced as a trainer, you will discover the balance that works for you. Prepare the stage well, present yourself with care, and the performance should follow.

### TOOLKIT CHECKLIST

When planning your training course, you can now ask yourself the following questions.

- ■  Have I thought about the first impressions my participants will have of me?
- ▾  Have I considered how to set expectations for behaviour?
- ▦  Have I planned my sessions so that all participants feel included?
- ●  Have I taken care with the style and difficulty of language I am using?
- ■  Have I used presentation software purposefully?

# PART C
# TRAINING ACTIVITIES

## IN THESE THREE CHAPTERS YOU WILL:

- find 50 activities to use in training sessions;
- get a feel for what works as starter, middle or end activities;
- consider the resources you will need;
- see that certain activities are more suitable as individual, pair or group work.

All trainers are different. In this part of the book we have included a wide range of activities so you can choose ones that will work for you. We have tried and tested all of the activities we have included, or we have seen them work very effectively in training courses we have attended. Some you will recognise, some will be new. You may have seen other versions of them before.

We have grouped them into three categories: ones you could use at the start, in the middle or at the end of a session. It is up to you, though, to decide when best to use them, adapting each to your own style and context.

Under the description of each activity, we have included some possible 'participant talk', and occasionally 'trainer talk', to give you further guidance should you need it.

# 9
# AT THE START

## KEY WORDS IN THIS CHAPTER

- activities
- at the start
- relationships
- participants

- engage
- enthuse
- training

## IN THIS CHAPTER YOU WILL:

The purpose of the 16 activities in this chapter is to:

- build relationships with and between participants;
- engage with participants' prior knowledge;
- enthuse participants and get them onside.

## 1. NAME CHALLENGE

Learning participants' names at the start of a training session can help you build good relationships. If you have fewer than 20 participants, you can learn their names quickly. Ask the first person to tell the group their name and their favourite colour, place, etc. Then ask the second person to do the same, but also to remind the group about the first person. This continues, with each new person telling the group about themselves and all the previous people.

   This activity is for your whole group.

**'My name is Jan and my favourite colour is pink; this is Jayshree, and her favourite colour is magenta.'**

## 2. HELLO IN YOUR LANGUAGE

If you have an international or multicultural audience, and your participants speak a number of different languages, this is a great starter activity. As they enter, or when they're sitting down, walk around the audience, asking them to tell you how to say 'hello' in their language, along with their name. They feel valued by you asking about their language, you connect to others by using their language, and you can refer to participants by name during your training.

This activity is for your whole group.

*'Bonjour, ciao, ni hao, selamat pagi, guten tag, buna.'*

## 3. GUESS WHAT, GUESS WHO

You may have done something similar to this activity at a party!

Without them seeing what is written on it, give each participant a sticky note to hold on their forehead or back (depending on how adhesive the sticky note is!), telling them not to look at it. The participants have to guess by asking other people closed questions (yes/no) about what is written on their own sticky note.

For example, if you are leading a course about drama, the sticky notes could be names of famous actors. Alternatively, each sticky note could represent a role at a school (e.g. teacher, student, parent). What you choose may be related to what comes next in your training course.

You need at least one pre-prepared sticky note per person.

This activity is for your whole group.

*'Am I a woman? Am I still alive? Am I American . . . ?'*

*'Do I hold a senior role in the school? Do I spend most of my time in an office?'*

## 4. WHAT IS YOUR FAVOURITE?

Ask participants to choose their favourite number, word, object, colour, etc. Ask them to explain their choice to the other group members. After a few minutes take one example from each group and ask them to share with the whole group. This gives an opportunity for the whole group to 'bond' with each other – even if their choices may be a little bizarre!

You don't need any resources for this activity, although you could always write on mini-whiteboards or sticky notes.

This activity includes individual, small-group and whole-group work.

*'My favourite number is the number 13 because it is an odd number, but also a happy number.'*

## 5. TWO TRUTHS AND A LIE

Before using this activity decide if it is appropriate for your audience, as some participants may be uncomfortable with telling a lie.

Ask each participant to share two truths and one lie about themselves to the members of their group. The groups then need to decide which facts are true and which are not. This activity encourages lots of talk and often laughter, as participants quickly discover interesting facts about their peers.

You don't need any resources for this activity, although you could always ask participants to record on mini-whiteboards or sticky notes.

This activity includes individual, small-group and whole-group work.

*'I live in the UK, I have a 15-year-old daughter and I fly hot-air balloons.'*

## 6. FACTS ABOUT ME

Ask each participant to share one fact about themselves. It can be about anything, but encourage people to be brave!

Give each group time to share facts with their peers before asking them to decide which fact to share with the whole group. This activity usually encourages participants to ask follow-up questions about the facts, which stimulates lively discussion.

You don't need any resources for this activity.

This activity includes individual, small-group and whole-group work.

*'My fact is that I once canoed on one of the Great Lakes in North America.'*

## 7. LOCATION, LOCATION, LOCATION

Ask participants in small groups to tell each other where they currently live, a place they have visited recently and the place they would most like to visit.

This activity often encourages people to offer stories and reasons for their choices, which encourages a positive group dynamic.

It can be helpful (but not essential) to provide a map of the world for each group.

This activity includes individual and small-group work.

*'I live in Geneva, I recently visited Shenzhen and I would most like to go to Quito because . . .'*

## 8. CLOCKING IN

This is an easy way to get participants to know and work with each other. Give each of them a piece of paper with a clock face drawn on it showing the positions of 12, 3, 6 and 9 o'clock. Ask the participants to stand up and quickly introduce themselves to other participants, fixing 'appointments' with one other person for each of the four times (making sure they write down each other's names).

All participants should then have four ready-made pairs for when you ask them to do activities either immediately or throughout the session or day. Simply ask them to work with their '3 o'clock appointment' for one activity, another for their '6 o'clock', etc.

All you need to prepare is enough copies of the clock face. Alternatively, ask them to draw it themselves on a piece of scrap paper.

This activity is for everyone in the group.

*'Do you already have a 3 o'clock appointment? No? Let's both write each other's name down for 3 o'clock.'*

## 9. HOT SEAT

This activity introduces the key ideas in the training by making participants think about their own prior knowledge. Choose a volunteer from your audience. Give them a card with a key word or picture which relates to the topic of the training. Only allow this volunteer to see the card. Ask everyone else to direct questions to the volunteer in the 'hot seat' (you can put a chair at the front of the room) to work out what is written on the card. The volunteer can only answer 'yes' or 'no'.

This activity is for the whole group.

*[On the card: Assessment.] 'Does it happen in classrooms? Yes. Is it solely the teacher's responsibility? No. Does it only involve writing? No. Does it . . . ?'*

## 10. WORD PAIRS

This activity gets participants to talk and engage with key ideas for the training, making their prior knowledge explicit. Prepare in advance cards with pairs of words written on them. You need to prepare each card twice so that more than one person will have a card with the same pair of words on it.

Give each person a pair of words, distributing them so that each card is duplicated elsewhere in the room. Ask participants to think about what links/connects the two words and in what ways they are different. Next, ask them to find another person who has the same pair of words as them and to discuss their ideas together.

This activity begins as an individual activity and ends as a pair activity.

You will need to prepare cards with pairs of words on them.

*[On the card: Active/Passive.] 'I think these words are different because . . .'*

## 11. BASKET OF OBJECTS

Giving participants a basket of objects always causes a flurry of excitement! You may want to approach this activity in a very open-ended way and ask participants to think about what the objects represent in relation to your training focus. Alternatively, you may want to provide some direction and ask how the objects may be used to enhance active learning, assessment for learning, creative thinking, etc.

You will need at least one basket of objects, perhaps more if you want to do this activity in small groups. The basket could include objects such as mini-whiteboards, rulers and erasers, or it could include objects such as mirrors, wooden spoons, a leaf.

This activity can be done in pairs or as small-group or whole-group work.

*'With this mini-whiteboard we can instantly check how many students have the right answer.'*

*'This mirror could be used when we are asking students to reflect on how they have responded to the task.'*

## 12. RANK YOURSELF / LINES OF CONFIDENCE / STAND IN A CORNER

This activity helps participants to get to know each other and/or for you to find out how much they know about a particular topic.

Ask participants to stand up and arrange themselves in order along one wall of the training room. You can choose different ways in which to create that order. For example, they could order themselves alphabetically by first name, by how much they think they employ active learning strategies or even simply by height. They get to talk to each other in the process. Once they are lined up, you can talk to the people at different points of the line to find out why they are there.

You could also ask them to divide into groups (stand in a nominated corner) rather than rank themselves (for example, by subject group or by whether they like or dislike particular teaching and learning activities).

No materials are needed for this activity, but you will need enough space in the room and clear areas for participants to stand.

This activity is for your whole group.

*'I'm going to stand to the left of you because it sounds from what you are saying that I take longer to prepare my lessons.'*

## 13. PHOTOCOPIER

Place a picture or diagram at the front of the room, facing away from participants (perhaps stuck to the back of a chair or flipchart). Divide your participants into groups of four, all sitting around their own table. Instruct them to decide who is going to be Runner 1 and Runner 2 and who is going to draw.

When you say 'go', Runner 1 should run to the front, memorise the picture for ten seconds, run back to their group and tell the Drawer what to draw to replicate the picture. The Drawer is not allowed to ask questions; the Runner is not allowed to draw! After three minutes tell Runner 2 to do the same thing. This time the Drawer can ask questions, but again only has three minutes to complete the picture.

After this, the fourth member of the group should bring their pictures to the front. You can then review the pictures and draw out the key features of the drawing you want them to focus on. This activity also helps groups to get to know each other.

You need one large sheet of plain paper and a black marker pen for each group. You also need the picture or diagram to be copied.

This activity includes small-group and whole-group work.

*'In the picture there is a classroom with children sitting in rows, listening to a teacher who is standing at the front with a book in their hand . . .'*

## 14. SEE–THINK–WONDER

This is an excellent starter activity that is also a useful thinking routine. Find an interesting picture related to the topic you are talking about and either project it onto a screen or have sufficient copies for participants to see it and work together.

Give them strictly three or four minutes only for each of the three parts of the routine. Ask them in groups to (a) describe what they see; (b) reflect on what they have described; (c) think of questions arising from their description and reflection. Monitor the participants closely so that they do not stray onto the next part of the routine before they have finished the previous one – you may need to train them to do this properly.

Once they have seen, thought and wondered, invite one group at a time to report back in the same order – again not allowing them to stray into the next part of the routine. The picture can then be used as a stimulus for more work or to lead into the next activity on something related to the picture.

It is important to provide a high-quality, suitable image for this activity. Make sure you acknowledge copyright if the image is not your own.

This is a group or pair activity.

*Trainer: 'What can you see?' Participant: 'There is a building with high walls and not many windows – I think it might be a prison.' Trainer: 'You think it might be a prison?' Participant: 'Sorry, that is for later. I can see a man . . .'*

## 15. COGNITION THROUGH DRAWING

Many adults are not comfortable with drawing. Research suggests, however, that even the most basic of art skills can help unlock thinking or explain difficult ideas.

Start with a warm-up exercise of drawing stick people doing different activities, then ask the participants to draw something more complex, perhaps even an abstract concept like metacognition or something hard to convey in their subject area, e.g. how to talk in French about things that happened in the past. In pairs, participants should then try to describe the other person's drawing. This will help people both refine their explanation or understanding and hopefully learn something as well.

Participants need sufficient paper and pens.

This activity works best when people work with a partner who will not judge them on how well they draw!

*'In your picture, I can see a student thinking again and again about the same problem but getting stuck because they don't know any other methods to use.'*

## 16. ONLINE QUIZ

Most, if not all, of your participants will have brought smartphones, tablets or computers to the training room. Make sure they are online, then ask them to log onto a site such as Kahoot, where you will already have created a quiz for your participants related to your topic. The easiest quiz type to use is multiple choice. Design a series of questions to test their knowledge of a topic.

A site like Kahoot provides graphics and music to make the quiz feel both like fun and that there is something at stake. Participants can see after each question whether they were right and how well they are doing relative to other people in the group. You as the trainer can quickly gauge the prior knowledge of individuals and the group as a whole. If you are feeling generous, you could give the winner a prize!

This activity needs preparation. Try **www.kahoot.com**, where you can learn to design and use quizzes for free. Check internet connectivity before you begin.

This activity is intended to involve everyone. If some people are not able to get online, they will have to answer in a pair with someone else.

*'In this syllabus, how many learning objectives are there? How many written exams are there for this syllabus? Which of these four is an optional topic?'*

# 10

# IN THE MIDDLE

## KEY WORDS IN THIS CHAPTER

- in the middle
- reflection
- learning
- thinking

- discussion
- collaboration
- engagement

### IN THIS CHAPTER YOU WILL:

*The purpose of the 22 activities in this chapter is to:*

- help participants reflect on their work as professionals;
- learn from each other;
- encourage thinking;
- stimulate discussion and collaboration.

### 17. KWL GRIDS

Create a three-column table, with the three columns headed 'What I know' (K), 'What I want to know' (W) and 'What I learned' (L). Participants should complete the first two columns at the start of the training and the final column at the end of the training. This helps them to take ownership of their own learning and feel more involved in the training. You will need to print off the KWL grids beforehand.

This is an activity where participants work individually.

*'I know . . . and I want to know . . .'*

## 18. DISCUSSION

To enable participants to build on their prior knowledge, and think about your objectives in relation to their practice, it is important that you build in opportunity for them to engage in discussion. There are lots of different approaches, some of which are given below.

- Discuss in pairs.
- Pairs to fours – start work in pairs, and then share ideas in a group of four.
- Envoys – a group undertakes a task and then an envoy from each group moves to a new group to explain and summarise the group's approach. The new group explains their approach and the envoy takes their ideas back to the original group.
- Snowball – pairs discuss, double up to fours, which double up to eights. One representative of each eight then shares ideas with the whole class.
- Rainbow – after small groups have discussed, each group member is given a colour. Participants with the same colour have to join up into new groups. In their new groups, each participant shares the discussion from the original group.

This activity takes place in pairs or as a group.

*'In my pair we thought that . . .'*

## 19. STICKY NOTES

Sticky notes can be used in many different ways to focus and facilitate thinking and discussion. You could ask participants to record an idea, comment on a video clip they have just watched, share their favourite resource or activity or generate lots of words around a particular topic. It is useful to ask participants only to note one word or idea per sticky note so that they can compare and group them according to follow-up tasks.

You will need packs of sticky notes. We like to use different colours, sizes and shapes! This activity includes individual, small-group and whole-group work.

*'On my sticky notes I have written . . .'*

## 20. CARD SORT

When you put an activity onto cards (rather than a handout, for example), it encourages a different type of interaction between participants. To start with, someone has to pick up the cards and read them while others may be thinking about how to sort them. Card sorts usually generate lots of discussion, perhaps because of the ease with which they can be moved, manipulated and shared out.

It can be useful not to provide too many instructions or parameters on how you would like the cards sorted and just observe how different pairs or groups do this. However, you could ask participants to match them, order them, spot the odd one(s) out, sort into two/three/four groups, etc.

After small groups have sorted the cards, decide if it is appropriate to share strategies and thoughts across the wider group.

You will need packs of cards for pairs or groups.

This activity includes individual, small-group and whole-group strategies.

***'We thought this card went well with that card because . . .'***

## 21. DIAMOND NINE

Ask participants in groups to brainstorm words or phrases about a topic and write each of them on separate sticky notes. Once they have exhausted their ideas, tell them they must select just nine of them, and then rank them in a diamond shape. The sticky note at the top of the diamond is the most important idea, and the one at the bottom the least important of the nine. The rows in between (2–3–2) are for the remaining ideas, meaning some can be ranked equally.

As a slight variation, you could ask them initially to come up with words individually and then share with the rest of their group, choosing the nine most frequently occurring or joint favourite words.

An extension to this activity could be to ask the participants to come up with a phrase including all nine words.

You will need sticky notes and pens for this activity.

This is a group activity, with some possible individual work at the beginning.

***'I think this word should go at the top because . . .'***

## 22. NORMING THE STORM

Put the participants into groups and ask them each to brainstorm a separate idea or question using sticky notes that they will place randomly on a large sheet of paper. After a few minutes, ask the group to swap their large sheet of paper with another group. Participants

*(Continued)*

(Continued)

in the other group with the new sheet of paper and idea or question in front of them should then try to categorise the sticky notes, adding more and keeping separate any sticky notes they are unsure about. The two groups then get together and talk through each idea or question in turn.

This activity requires large sheets of paper, lots of sticky notes and pens.

This is a group activity.

*'We can understand why you have put the words "speak" and "listen" together, but we don't know why "read" and "write" are not in a pair. Could you tell us?'*

## 23. TRAFFIC LIGHTS

This is a useful method for sifting ideas. Either ask participants to brainstorm ideas on a topic or give them a series of statements. Participants should then class them according to whether they think they are a bad idea (red), good idea (green) or if they are not sure yet (amber). Participants could alternatively classify with coloured stickers or by placing the ideas or statements on coloured pieces of paper posted on the wall so that they can then compare their feelings with those of other participants.

This activity requires stickers, sheets of paper or simply pens that are red, amber and green.

This is a group activity.

*'I agree that this should be in red because it is stopping us from being creative in our lesson planning. I'm not sure, though, that this should be in green because I don't agree that our head of department should always make the final decision about what we teach.'*

## 24. JIGSAW

This is a cooperative learning approach where all group members are dependent on each other to succeed. This strategy splits the task into smaller parts (often on cards). Each group member takes one card which they then share with each other. After hearing all the information, the group must decide which are the relevant pieces of information needed to solve the task and in which order.

You will need packs of cards for each small group.
This activity includes small-group work.

*'This task seems to be about how to write a policy on homework. I'm not sure, though, whether the audience is just teachers or parents as well. I think one of the other groups must have that piece of information.'*

## 25. ALWAYS, SOMETIMES, NEVER

Instead of asking questions this activity uses statements. Giving participants a statement rather than a question generates a different type of discussion, especially if the statements are not necessarily correct!

You may decide to give just one statement to discuss or more than one. In either case ask participants whether the statement is always true, sometimes true or never true. Whatever they decide they must prove or disprove it.

You will need statement cards for each pair or small group.
This activity includes pair or small-group work.

*'Children should learn how to do maths without a calculator.'*

*'Every science lesson needs to include a practical.'*

*'In geography, it is important to know how to read maps.'*

## 26. WHAT IS THE SAME? WHAT IS DIFFERENT?

Give participants two words, numbers, objects or pictures to compare. Ask them to notice what is the same and what is different. This activity encourages participants to notice details and think more deeply about an idea.

You don't need any resources for this activity unless you are using objects or pictures to compare.

This activity includes individual, pair, small-group and whole-group work.

*[The trainer shows a 3 and a 6 and asks what is the same and what is different.]*

*Participants: 'They are both single digit numbers; they are both below 10; they are both in the 3 times table; one is an odd number, the other even; one is below 5, the other above 5; one is a prime number, the other is not . . .'*

## 27. THIS IS THE ANSWER, WHAT IS THE QUESTION?

This activity is exactly as it sounds! Give participants the answer and ask them to discuss what they think the question could be. This is a great activity to show that there is often more than one solution and that often the answer is not the most important element of learning.

You don't need any resources for this activity.

This activity includes individual, pair, small-group and whole-group work.

*'The answer is 10. I think the question is . . .'*

## 28. ODD ONE OUT

Offer three examples to participants and ask them to discuss which is the odd one out. The point of this activity is the discussion and reasoning generated, rather than actually deciding which is the odd one out. Often, participants will argue that each example could be the odd one out!

You need three examples to give participants. These could be written on the board or given out on cards.

This activity includes individual, small-group and whole-group strategies.

*'I think green is the odd one out because . . .'*

## 29. SORT IT OUT

Ask participants to get into pairs or groups. Give them a blank or incomplete grid with headings on each of the columns and rows, and invite them to complete it using the cut-out, laminated words you supply in an envelope. The grid that you ask them to complete should be relevant to the topic you are covering.

You will need to prepare enough grids for the group and envelopes full of cut-out, laminated words. If you want to use the cut-out words again, make sure you ask the participants to put them back into the envelope at the end!

This activity takes place in groups or in pairs.

*'I think this word goes here because . . .'*

## 30. SORTING ADVANTAGES AND DISADVANTAGES

Give participants cards containing advantages and disadvantages. Participants should classify the cards into advantages and disadvantages. You could also ask them to distinguish between the most important and least important.

You need to prepare sufficient numbers of cards in advance.

This activity takes place as a group.

***'In my opinion, this is an advantage because . . .'***

## 31. GRAPHIC ORGANISERS

There are many different ways for participants to represent their knowledge graphically. These include approaches known as mind-mapping and concept-mapping to encourage participants to make connections or draw out contrasts between ideas. They also help participants to brainstorm and generate new ideas and integrate new ideas with existing understanding. You can see some examples below.

Participants need pens and paper. This activity could be undertaken by an individual, pair or small group.

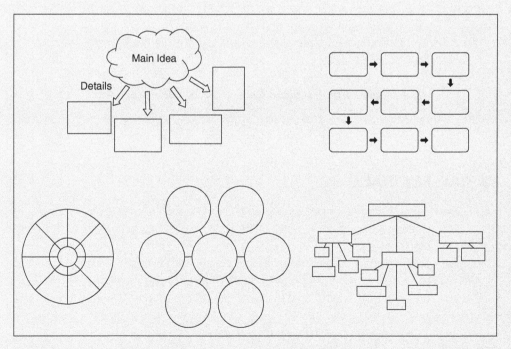

*(Continued)*

**Figure 10.1**   (Continued)

**Figure 10.1**   Examples of graphic organisers

## 32. HONEYCOMB

Cut out lots of hexagons in advance (you can find templates online) and give a big pile to each group. Ask them to write in the middle of each hexagon an idea or concept related to a specific topic and then invite them to connect these together using the sides of the hexagons. This will help them visualise and sort their ideas.

You may need to find a friend who will help you cut out the hexagons!

This is a group or pair activity.

*'If we place this hexagon here, it links with that idea.'*

## 33. GALLERY WALK

Post relevant ideas, thoughts or quotes on a topic around your training room, making sure there is sufficient space to move around. Invite your participants to look at each one in turn, noting their thoughts.

You will need to prepare in advance what you are going to post and have pins or white tack to stick the pieces of paper to the wall (make sure you have permission to do this!).

This starts as an individual or pair activity but can lead to group or plenary discussions.

*'When I look at this poster, it makes me wonder . . .'*

## 34. SILENT DEBATE

Either ask participants to answer a question in groups or on their own, writing their thoughts in one colour on a large piece of paper. Once they have given their answer, they should pass it to another group or person. This next group or person should add more thoughts or ask questions on the piece of paper. One or two more groups or people could then do the same.

Eventually the piece of paper returns to the original person or group and they can see how others responded to their initial thinking. Participants could either write on the pieces of paper at tables or the pieces of paper could be posted on the wall. It is a good idea to post all the pieces of paper on the wall at the end and then invite participants to do a 'gallery walk' and look at each final piece of paper in turn.

Participants will need large sheets of paper with topics written on them and a different coloured pen for each group or person.

This activity works best in groups but can be done individually or in pairs.

*'That's interesting. When I wrote that, I didn't think about . . .'*

## 35. MAKING A STATEMENT

Post a number of statements on posters or flipcharts around the room. Divide the group evenly so that an equal number of people go to look at just one of the statements. Give the participants a few minutes to think about that one statement. Then, ask them to seek as many opinions as possible from the other participants who have been looking at different statements.

After around ten minutes, ask the participants to return to their original statement and summarise on the piece of paper the opinions they have heard. They should then discuss what they have written with the other participants who were also originally looking at the same statement. To complete the activity, ask those standing next to each statement to present their summary to everyone else.

You will need to prepare several statements and post them around the room.

This activity includes individual, pair and group work, as well as a final plenary.

*'Do you agree that every lesson should include differentiation?'*

## 36. BARRIERS AND SOLUTIONS

This is a great activity that addresses not only the barriers that participants are often thinking about but also offers solutions to those barriers.

Give each small group one large piece of paper (flipchart paper works well) and a coloured marker pen. Ask each group to divide their paper into two halves and on one side record any potential barriers they can think of. After a few minutes ask groups to swap, moving in a clockwise direction. Each group must now try to offer possible solutions to the barriers posed. After a few minutes swap again, so that different groups can see the barriers but also offer their own solutions to them. Keep swapping until each group is in possession of their original piece of paper.

You may want to leave the activity there or discuss some of the barriers and solutions with the whole group. Whatever you decide it is useful to keep them displayed on the walls so participants can reflect on them further or perhaps take photographs.

You need some large pieces of paper with topics written on them and marker pens.

This activity includes small-group and whole-group work.

*'One solution to this barrier could be . . .'*

## 37. REVERSE ENGINEERING

Inventors or designers often pull an object apart to work out how it was put together. You can do the same with exam questions, items on a school policy or something similar. Give participants a small number of questions or statements to look at, and ask them to pull them apart. This can lead to lots of debate and a deeper appreciation of the importance of language.

This activity needs a list of questions or items for participants to discuss. They could all be given the same list and asked to choose which ones to look at. Alternatively, you could choose (for each group or pair) which ones you would like them to do, so that the list is more evenly distributed and all questions or items are covered.

This activity could take place in groups or pairs.

*'Why do you think this exam question has been worded in this way?'*

*'Why does the school have this rule?'*

# 38. SPEED SHARING

This is an activity to enable participants to share ideas with several other people.

Set up chairs in two circles opposite each other so that everyone has a partner. Each pair is going to be together for two minutes, during which time they will discuss some topic or a question provided by you. At the end of the two minutes ring a bell (or make another noise) at which point everyone moves one place to the left. They now have a new partner for the next three-minute discussion.

You need chairs and space, as well as a focus for each two-minute conversation. If you do not have space for two circles, arrange the chairs in two parallel lines, with people moving one place to the left each time, moving round to the other end of the row when they run out of chairs.

This activity involves participants working in pairs.

*'Hello, nice to meet you! The idea I would like to share with you is . . .'*

# 11
# AT THE END

## KEY WORDS IN THIS CHAPTER

- at the end
- summarise
- reflect
- identify
- outcomes

- actionable
- ideas
- take-away
- session

### IN THIS CHAPTER YOU WILL:

*The purpose of the 12 activities in this chapter is to:*

- summarise and reflect on the session;
- identify individual learning outcomes;
- provide actionable ideas to take away and use.

### 39. SIX-WORD HEADLINE

A 'six-word story' is a useful way to summarise at the end of an activity.

You don't need any resources for this activity; however, writing the words on a postcard or mini-whiteboard can work really well.

This activity can be an individual task or carried out as a pair or small group.

Once composed, share your six-word headlines with the rest of the group.

***'Useful for sorting and ranking ideas.'***

## 40. POSTCARDS (1)

Even with the best of intentions, participants often return to school and forget about the training they have just received. So, asking them to send a postcard to themselves is a fun way to remind themselves of all their good intentions.

At the end of the session give each participant a postcard on which they need to record what they are hoping to do, change and implement as a result of the training. Collect them in and then at some point after the event post them out! You may decide to post them immediately, or wait for up to three months. Either way, participants receive a little reminder about both the training and the outcomes they were hoping to achieve.

Remind them to include the address which they would like the postcard to be sent to!

You need a postcard for each participant.

This activity is an individual task.

*'Dear Me, I really enjoyed the training session today. Don't forget when you receive this to use the see–think–wonder activity . . .'*

## 41. POSTCARDS (2)

Ask the participants to evaluate the session on the back of a postcard. Because of the limited space available, participants really have to think about what to include and their choice of words.

You could invite a few participants to read out their postcard evaluations. Or you could simply collect them in and read rhem at your leisure after the event.

You need a postcard for each participant.

This activity is an individual task.

*'I liked the way you facilitated discussion and gave everybody a voice.'*

## 42. EXIT TICKETS

Distribute to everyone in the group an attractively designed ticket or card. Ask them before they leave to write one or more ideas that they are going to use tomorrow, next week or during the next month. If participants write something down, they are more likely to do it, especially if the ticket or card looks nice in which case they might keep it on their desk or wall.

Either download or design your own ticket or card for the participants.

This is an individual activity.

*'I will use more pair and group work.'*

## 43. ONE TAKE-AWAY

This is a very easy and simple way of asking participants to summarise the training and what they will do with it. Ask each participant to think of the one key 'take-away' they are going to use or implement as a result of the training. Depending on numbers, you could either go around the whole group and ask every participant for feedback, or if numbers are too big, ask participants to share as a group and then perhaps take one example from each.

You don't need any resources for this activity but you might like to ask participants to make a record on sticky notes.

This activity is an individual task.

**'My take-away is that I'm not always going to share the learning objectives with my students at the beginning of the lesson.'**

## 44. HEAD, HEART, BIN, TRY

Ask participants individually to consider which aspect of the training has made them think (head), which aspect of the training they have loved (heart), one aspect they would like to bin and one aspect they would like to try.

Bring the participants together to offer examples under each heading. This activity helps participants to understand that they do not need to implement all of the training and also allows them to see which parts their colleagues found relevant or not.

You don't need any resources for this activity but you might like to ask participants to make a record on sticky notes. These could then be stuck onto a larger sheet or board under each section.

This activity is an individual task.

**'I think . . . I love . . . I wouldn't use . . . but I would . . .'**

## 45. 10, 10, 10

Sometimes, reflecting on the training can seem a little overwhelming for those participants who want to implement everything – tomorrow! So, this activity allows participants to see that there is another way. Ask participants to think individually about what they would like to implement or try out over the next 10 days, 10 weeks and 10 months.

You don't need any resources for this activity but you might like to ask participants to record their actions on sticky notes or paper.

This activity is an individual task.

**'In the next 10 days, I will . . . Over the next 10 months, I will . . .'**

## 46. LIST 5

Participants should list five things they have learnt during the training. They should team up with other participants, pooling their lists together, and each identifying five action points they will implement as a result of the training.

You don't need to prepare any resources for this activity.

This activity takes place in a group.

*'The top 5 things I have learnt from today are . . .'*

## 47. WHAT HAPPENS NEXT?

Write on the board the list of objectives for the course, and ask the question 'What happens next?' Participants should identify their next steps, having learnt (or at least engaged with) each objective. When all participants have had a chance to decide on their answer, ask for some suggestions and discuss what action participants will take to achieve their next steps.

This activity takes place individually and then as a group.

*'I have learnt more about to how run effective plenary sessions.*
*The first thing I will do when I am next preparing*
*a lesson with a plenary will be . . .'*

## 48. BULL'S EYE

Take a picture of a dartboard with you and pin it up at the end of the session. Read out the objectives of the training and ask participants to run to the front to mark on the dartboard how well each objective was achieved. If the objective was achieved well, they should place a mark in the bull's eye in the centre of the board. If poorly achieved, they should place a mark at the edge of the dart board. Use the dartboard to discuss ideas for follow-on training.

You will need a picture (or projection) of a dartboard. Make sure that wherever you place (or project) the dartboard, it is somewhere that can have marks placed on it.

This activity takes place in a group.

*'I'm putting this in the centre because . . .'*

## 49. QUICK QUESTIONS

In pairs, participants prepare four quick questions about the content of the training. Each question should begin with one of the words: What, When, Why or How. Participants must be able to answer their question correctly. They then swap questions with another pair and answer them.

You do not need to prepare any resources for this activity.

This activity takes place as a pair, and then as a group.

*'What was the most important thing we learnt in session one?'*

## 50. RANKING

You may have employed a similar activity at the start (see *Activity 12*), so it will be interesting to see how many participants feel the training has been transformative.

Clear or find a large space and invite participants to stand in different areas of the room, according to how confident they now feel about different topics as a result of training.

No materials are needed for this activity – just sufficient space.

This is an activity for the whole group.

*'I'm putting myself between you and you because . . .'*

You will of course come across plenty of other activities you can use in your training sessions. If you are a teacher, you can adapt many of the activities you use with children for working with adults. Be aware, though, that some participants may be less keen to get up and move around, or even talk to each other (at least before you break the ice and gain their confidence)!

Keep a bank of possible activities that you can look through, prior to each training session that you lead – and that you can keep handy to use as an alternative during training. It is sensible to have some activities in mind that require very little resource in case technology breaks down or materials you asked to be printed have not arrived. Remember that the best trainers are adaptable and flexible – and carry around with them in their heads (or in their bags) a large toolkit of training ideas!

## TOOLKIT CHECKLIST

When planning your training course, you can now ask yourself the following questions.

- Have I chosen which activities I could use in my training sessions and at which stage?
- Have I understood the importance of knowing and using a variety of activities?
- Have I thought about the preparation and resources I will require?

# EVALUATING AND REFLECTING ON YOUR TRAINING AND DEVELOPING YOURSELF AS A TRAINER

# 12

# SELF-EVALUATION

## KEY WORDS IN THIS CHAPTER

- evidence
- feedback
- impact

- negative
- positive
- self-evaluation

### IN THIS CHAPTER YOU WILL:

- think about how to reflect upon and evaluate individual training sessions;
- think about how to evaluate the impact of your training at different levels;
- consider the most appropriate forms of evidence to support your evaluation;
- learn how to deal positively with negative evaluation feedback.

## EVALUATING TRAINING

If you want to improve your training, you need to evaluate it.

First, let's talk about the kind of evaluation you should do immediately after a training session has finished. When you finish a training session, you will often have ideas about 'how it went'. Write those ideas down straightaway – don't wait until later, you'll forget.

Once you get back home, or to your hotel, use what you have written down to *think* about what you would do the same or differently next time.

- You could make two lists: 'what went well (WWW)?' and what 'could be better (CBB)?'
- You could ask yourself: 'Did they learn what I wanted them to learn?' And then ask yourself: 'If so, why? If not, why not? How do I know?'
- You could ask yourself 'Why?' and 'How?' about each idea you wrote down after the session, and then keep asking 'Why' or 'How' until you have worked out what to do next time.

*I've used the Why? and How? technique on a number of occasions; it really helps me to break down participants' feedback, and work out how to respond to it.*

*On one occasion when training abroad, I realised that even though I had given clear instructions, many participants did not start the task, continued to chat, and appeared confused about what they were supposed to do. I wrote about it immediately after my training session. Later, I went through the Why?/How? process:*

*'Participants had to use what I told them to complete the activity, but many seemed confused and didn't get started straightaway.'*

*WHY? Maybe they didn't understand the instructions.*
*WHY? Perhaps I hadn't explained slowly enough.*
*HOW Would I change it? Make sure I speak more slowly, and put the instructions on a PowerPoint slide.*
*WHY? Because they'd be able to spend time reading the instructions and making sure they understood them without having to wait for me to come round.*

*It seems simple (and is!), but it helps me to be explicit about what I do well and what needs to change. On another occasion, I was running a keynote session at a conference. I very rarely talk a lot during keynotes, but I ask a lot of questions, and give my audience tasks. Here's my immediate thoughts (and the Why?/How? process afterwards).*

*'Participants got stuck in straightaway – I was surprised how willing they were to volunteer answers right from the start.'*

*WHY? Perhaps it's because I greeted them all individually at the door.*
*HOW did that work? Because I greeted them, I established a relationship with them and they didn't feel threatened – they felt like the questions were an extension of the conversations I'd already had with them.*
*WHY else? It may also have been because I asked open questions which allowed them to draw on their own experience, making the training relevant for them immediately.*

**TAKE A MOMENT**

Think about the last training session you ran or the last lesson you taught. Follow the process above: write down your initial ideas about how the training session went and then ask yourself 'Why?' and 'How?' for each of the ideas.

These kinds of evaluation are important. Having this kind of internal conversation with your-self is essential to help you think about your training. Thinking about your training will help you to improve it.

Chapman (2015) describes a really useful model to help you think about your ability as a trainer. When you start training, you may be an unconscious incompetent. You are not very good at training, but you don't realise it. To improve, you need to become conscious of your incompetence.

This is where evaluation really helps. Making yourself think about your training sessions, identifying good things, bad things and ways forward, is part of becoming conscious of your incompetence and gradually growing into a conscious competent. Gradually, as you gain more experience, your competence will become almost intuitive and you'll become an unconscious competent.

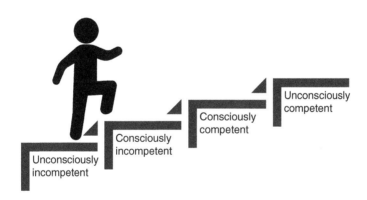

**Figure 12.1**   Levels of competence

## EVALUATING IMPACT WITH EVIDENCE

So, you want to move from unconscious incompetent through to unconscious competent? When you develop your practice, you do so through a reflective cycle: making changes to your practice, collecting evidence and reflecting consciously and critically upon the evidence, before deciding what you would do differently next time.

Evaluation evidence is important to this reflective cycle. The evidence you collect must give you information about your impact. Gut feeling is not enough – the way in which participants *appear* to respond during your training may be quite different to the judgement they make when undertaking a formal evaluation.

So, rather than just collecting evaluation data because your school or organisation requires it (to judge the efficacy of the course and participants' learning), think about what evidence you need to investigate *your* impact and so to improve the course or your practice more generally.

Impact can happen on different levels – a helpful framework comes from Guskey (2000). We have adapted and summarised Guskey's framework in the lists below.

We suggest these four levels of evaluation:

1. Participants' reactions.
2. Participants' learning.
3. Participants' use of new knowledge and skills, including students' learning outcomes.
4. Organisational change (adapted) at different levels.


## 1. WHAT WERE PARTICIPANTS' INITIAL IMPRESSIONS?

Participants' reactions to the training may be quite varied. You could investigate the answers to some of the following questions.

- Did they enjoy it?
- Was it worth their time, relevant and useful?
- Did it make sense?
- How good was your delivery?
- Can they suggest improvements to environment (food, lighting, seats, etc.)?

You can use the following sources of evidence:

- questionnaires;
- focus groups;
- interviews.


## 2. DID PARTICIPANTS LEARN?

Participants may be expected to learn new knowledge or skills, depending on the focus of the training.

You could investigate their learning through some of the following sources of evidence:

- participants' analysis of case studies where they must use their learning to interpret, for example, a classroom event;
- demonstration of skills in a simulation, for example planning a lesson in which their new learning is embedded and presenting it to the group;
- other evidence from participants' personal reflections (for example, through interviews, focus groups or questionnaires) or portfolios created during the course.

## 3. DID PARTICIPANTS USE THEIR LEARNING?

A training course is only worthwhile if participants do something with what they have learnt. You should be interested in the extent of implementation (how much they do it) and the quality of implementation (how well they do it, and did it achieve their aims, e.g. in students' learning?).

You can investigate the implementation of their learning through some of the following sources of evidence:

- classroom observations;
- questionnaires for teachers and students;
- interviews, possibly with a video of a lesson, asking the teacher to explain their actions;
- student attainment data;
- oral and written personal reflections.

## 4. WHAT WAS THE IMPACT ON THE ORGANISATION?

Understanding the impact of the training beyond the teacher and beyond their classroom is important. It usually requires talking to different people at different levels of the organisation to really trace through any impacts.

You may want to investigate:

- What was the impact on the school?
- What was the impact on the subject department?
- What was the impact on the teaching staff?
- What was the impact on climate and procedures?

You can use the following sources of evidence:

- minutes of staff and departmental meetings;
- questionnaires;
- focus groups;
- interviews.

*The first training course I facilitated was about using technology in classroom teaching. The immediate feedback I had about the workshop was really good, and I didn't really know why. It was not until much later that I realised. There are four important things to tell you first.*

*1.  Teachers were taught skills, such as how to use applications and how to structure learning activities and use them in class.*
*2.  Teachers used those skills to develop their own learning activities for their own lessons.*
*3.  Teachers worked independently or in pairs on computers, and I circulated to support them.*
*4.  All of the school staff attended the workshop over a series of three days.*

*Without realising it, I had set up structures which targeted each level of evaluation. At Level 1, participants enjoyed the course and responded well because they could see its relevance. They worked independently on computers and so had time to develop their skills and understanding with my support as I circulated around the room. They could also make decisions about the skills and understanding they wanted to develop. All of the school staff attended the workshop; this led to continued conversations about technology and the establishment of a 'technology learning' group across the whole school. Because participants created learning activities for use in their own classrooms, they were able to use their new knowledge and skills and feel confident in being able to do so.*

You can read more about the different types of evidence below. Think about whether each evidence source is appropriate for evaluating an outcome (for example, 'Did the activity change participants' thinking?') or a process (for example, 'How did the activity change participants' thinking?').

## IMMEDIATE ORAL AND WRITTEN PERSONAL REFLECTIONS

These include feedback provided by participants immediately after the training or during the training itself. These are mostly informal so you may ask participants to:

- write three words on a sticky note to provide feedback on today's course;
- give the course a mark out of 10, and write one sentence to justify your score;
- write down three 'what went well' ideas and one 'could be better'.

These are useful for gaining immediate feedback. You should treat the feedback with caution; if your participants are happy at the end of the day, they will tell you positive things. It may be that points for development only come to mind later that day, or a few days later. Indeed, a participant's feedback could easily have been influenced by the menu, the person they sat next to, the weather, or even how busy the roads were that morning.

## QUESTIONNAIRES

Questionnaires allow you to collect a lot of data from a lot of people quickly. However, to ensure your participants complete their questionnaires, it can be useful to issue them on paper or provide an incentive for them to complete an online questionnaire.
   You can ask:

- *Open* questions, which allow participants to provide long answers, using their own words. Questions starting with *how* and *why* usually give you more useful information to help develop your practice. For example:
   o   How did the discussion activity change your ideas about assessment for learning?
   o   Why did you choose this activity as your favourite part of the course?
- *Closed* questions, which allow participants to respond to a set of possible answers, for example yes/no, making selections from a number of options, or Likert-style questions where participants rate their agreement with a statement on a scale of 1 to 5. Questions starting with *which, to what extent* and *how much* are useful here. For example:
   o   To what extent did you learn from your peers?
   o   Which activity did you prefer?
   o   How much will the outcomes from today influence your classroom practice?

## INDIVIDUAL INTERVIEWS

These can be informal conversations or more formal interviews (although still quite short!). They are useful:

- when you want to explore something in depth with more than simple answers;
- to gain information in cases where the questions need explaining.

Just like in a questionnaire, questions can be closed (like a spoken questionnaire) or more open and conversational. It can be helpful to record the interview, so you can listen to it again later. If you are trying to provide evidence for the effectiveness of your training, then quoting what your participants say can be useful. If you cannot record the interview, just take notes instead.

Think about making your questions quite 'open' – ideas which you had not previously considered may emerge. Usually, you will not have the time or opportunity for formal interviews. However, if you are working within school, you may opt for something in the middle, sitting down in the staff room with one of your participants during a free period and chatting to them about your training. Remember though that people can be very polite, and you may get more honest feedback through the other approaches mentioned here.

## FOCUS GROUP DISCUSSIONS

Focus groups are usually conducted in groups of five or more. You should think of a number of prompt questions about the training or the implementation of what they have learnt from the training. The aim is to make conversation happen so you can really find out what your participants think and what they learnt.

Focus group discussion also helps you to judge whether particular pieces of feedback are supported by just one participant or by many. However, be careful of allowing strong-minded personalities to take over. You should try to avoid closed questions and ask open questions instead, for example, 'Who would like to talk about this part of the training?' or 'Can someone talk about an example of how the training has affected their practice?'

## MEASUREMENTS OF LEARNING

If you are training participants in a particular technique or a particular topic, you may be able to measure their perception of their skills and understanding before the training and then after the training (like the boarding and landing cards in this book).

If they are teachers, and you have taught them a new approach to teaching a particular topic, their own students' test scores may even be useful to you. If you are evaluating a longer programme, you may find questionnaires useful which measure more complex constructs like self-efficacy. However, an increase in test data does not necessarily prove that your training was *responsible* for any change; it may have happened anyway. Using more than one source of evidence together can help to confirm the impact of your training.

## DOCUMENT ANALYSIS

If you are evaluating at higher levels, minutes of meetings can often tell you how much your training has impacted discussions, attitudes and practice in schools. They reveal the thinking of different members of staff and can help identify obstacles and enablers to implementation of new ideas.

## OBSERVING AND EVALUATING

Observations also provide excellent evidence of impact. During and after a workshop you can write down your immediate reflections, and you may ask a colleague to write down their ideas about the workshop.

If you are evaluating at higher levels, then you may make observations in a classroom to investigate whether a teacher's practice has actually been affected by your training. For example, to explore the impact of a training course on dialogic teaching, you may watch a lesson, using a tick-list to record the different types of dialogue which you hear in the lesson. We will look more closely at observations in **Chapter 13**.

Watching lessons is just one way in which you can collect observational data. You may also observe staff or departmental meetings, you may accompany a teacher during the day, listening to and making notes about their conversations with colleagues, or you may make observations about the physical appearance of the school or its facilities.

## TAKE A MOMENT

Think about the different types of observation you may need in order to gain evidence for evaluation at each different level.

Finally, you may find that the organisation for whom you are training has a set of Standards, which your training has to meet (see **Chapter 14**). If a set of Standards helps you to think of targets to develop your practice, this is great. However, do not just be driven by the Standards. Look at what your observer and participants say about your training and develop targets from the evaluation evidence you have collected.

# WHAT HAPPENS IF FEEDBACK IS NEGATIVE?

Getting negative feedback is never a nice feeling, so it is important to think about how to respond to it. Sometimes, the feedback is about something which is beyond your control (see **Chapter 1**). Sometimes, it can be tempting to blame the participant ('Most of them liked it! What was wrong with him/her?'). But try to reframe the way in which you listen to and respond to feedback. Look at the ideas in Table 12.1.

**Table 12.1**   Responding to negative feedback

| |
|---|
| See all feedback as an opportunity. If it's good, it tells you what worked. If it's bad, it tells you how to make it better. Either way, it will be better next time! |
| Think about what it tells you for the longer term. How can you learn from this feedback, because that will improve your practice next time, the time after that, and beyond. |
| If you made a mistake, and you know about it, don't let it tear you apart. We can't have perfect days every day! This is important to stop you losing confidence. |
| Try to place yourself in your audience's shoes. For example, the room may have been so big that you hadn't realised the people at the back could not hear you. Or maybe they'd been to a very similar training course very recently – and you were trying to do the same things with them only a few weeks later. |
| If you really cannot understand the feedback, talk to the person involved. They may simply be more willing to express grievances and they may actually have been quite content. |
| If anybody is very rude, ignore them. The only valuable feedback is constructive feedback which is well expressed. |

## TAKE A MOMENT

Think back to feedback you have received before on your training or teaching. Did you see it as an opportunity? If so, what changes did you make to your practice? If not, what changes could you have made that would have improved your practice?

## TOOLKIT CHECKLIST

When planning your training course, you can now ask yourself the following questions.

- Have I thought about my own strategy for immediate evaluation of my training sessions?
- Have I understood the characteristics of different types of evaluation evidence and chosen appropriate evidence to evaluate my training at different levels?
- Have I understood how evaluation evidence is important to my own self-development?
- Have I made a plan for how to respond to negative feedback?

# 13

# OBSERVING AND BEING OBSERVED

## KEY WORDS IN THIS CHAPTER

- observation
- mentoring
- coaching
- support
- focus

- notes
- evidence
- others
- challenge

## IN THIS CHAPTER YOU WILL:

- learn how to observe and be observed as a trainer;
- explore the basics of mentoring and coaching;
- look at how you could support others who are, or who would like to be, trainers;
- consider how to plan training sessions with other trainers.

If you want to develop as a trainer, you need to make time both to observe and be observed.

If you are a teacher, you will almost certainly have been observed on numerous occasions. An inspector or your school principal may have observed you. If you are fortunate, a supportive colleague will have observed you and perhaps also acted as your coach or mentor. You may even have carried out a lesson study with other teachers, which is a little like a collaborative action research project.

In this chapter, we are going to look at how best to plan for observations – both as the person being observed and the person doing the observing. We will explore the basics of coaching and mentoring. In due course, you may play the role of mentor, coach or trainer of trainers. You may also team up with, or work alongside, other trainers. We will consider all of these situations while recalling throughout that the focus should remain on the *training* rather than the *trainer*.

# OBSERVATIONS

Many people get nervous when someone observes them. They may not have slept well the night before, they may have over-prepared, they may feel like they need to 'put on a show' and pretend to be someone they are not. This can lead to a great performance, but it can often mean you stumble through activities, talk too fast or rapidly forget your objectives.

Unless you practise mindfulness techniques, there is no easy way to overcome anxiety, especially if the observation is 'high stakes' and someone is evaluating whether you meet a specific standard to gain accreditation (more about this in **Chapter 14**).

If, however, the observation is for professional development reasons, there is a lot you can do to prepare well and reduce stress. It begins with finding an appropriate person to work with.

It is important that this person knows *how* to observe. This is the skill you are asking them to perform. It is up to you whether you think that person should also be an expert in the topic of your training, or whether you simply want them to observe. Be careful not to choose an observer based just on their years of experience. Such a person may have had many years as a trainer but not know how to observe or give you constructive feedback.

Knowledge of subject content might be crucial for an observation. If it is not, you may prefer to choose someone who can give you an insight from training in another subject area. If you are a teacher, you may already have seen the value of working with teachers from another department. It is beneficial as well to think about how you might reciprocate: is there something your observer can learn from you as well as something you can learn from them?

There are many developmental benefits of being observed as a trainer. For example, it can:

- help you discover a new way of doing something;
- provide another opinion when you are trying out something new;
- unpick why something is not working;
- give you time to reflect properly and with focus;
- reaffirm your skills as a trainer and boost your confidence.

The observer can benefit, too, and in similar ways. It allows you and your observer to think harder and articulate what it means to be a trainer, and to discuss both the challenges and the best ways of training.

There are three parts to a developmental observation:

- before – when the observer and person being observed agree on a focus;
- during – when the observer writes down any information relevant to the focus;
- after – when the observer and the person being observed meet to discuss.

# FOCUS

You should immediately notice the word 'focus'. It would not be practical to observe everything that occurs in a training session and make sense of it. When someone is observing you, or you are observing them, you should jointly agree what is 'in' and what is 'out'. You might, for example, ask someone to observe how effectively you use questioning in your training or to what extent you involve everyone in the group. You may want to observe how another trainer uses technology or how they break the ice. The focus could be on more than one area, and the possibilities are limitless but be realistic about what can be achieved and learnt from one observation.

## TAKE A MOMENT

Having read this book, write a list of specific areas you would like to observe in another trainer. Next, write a list of specific areas you think you would like another trainer to observe in you. How do these lists compare?

If you are unsure what to select as a focus, consider an aspect of one or more of the following.

- How clear are the objectives of my training session and do I stick to them?
- What purpose do my materials serve?
- How well do I use the environment in which I am training?
- How well do I interact with participants?
- How much variety is there in the activities I use?

You will notice that these five areas deliberately reflect the chapters in **Parts B** and **C** of this book. Take a look again at the Boarding Pass at the end of the **Introduction** as well.

Once you have agreed the focus, decide on the time and length of the observation, and create the conditions for success for both you and the observer. Make sure that the observer understands the context of the training, any prior learning and that he or she will feel welcome and comfortable in the training room.

# TAKING NOTES AND RECORDING EVIDENCE

When you are observing, there are a number of ways to record what you observe. The method you choose will depend on what you are observing, but the common element is to write something down as you will soon forget what happened even just a few minutes ago.

You could, for example:

- write a factual, objective description of what happens in the session, and highlight later the points that are most relevant to the focus of the observation;

- divide a piece of paper into two columns headed 'what went well' (WWW) and 'what could be better' (CBB), writing accordingly in each;
- observe the participants as a whole group but only note what a small number are doing;
- draw a picture of the training room and keep a record of how many times the trainer asks each participant or group a question;
- write a list of all the questions the trainer asks.

You may also find the quadrants in Table 13.1 useful to structure the feedback.

**Table 13.1**   Observation quadrants

| **Describe** | **Evaluate** |
|---|---|
| What did the trainer do? | How effective was it? |
| What did the participants do? | How can you tell? |
| *(What happened?)* | *(What went well?)* |
| 'You questioned the participants.' | 'You were good at asking questions.' |
| **Critical analysis** | **Implications** |
| Why was it effective? | How can the trainer improve? |
| Why was it ineffective? | What should you think about next time? |
| *(Why?)* | *(What could be better?)* |
| 'Your questioning was good because you paused before inviting a response.' | 'You could improve your questioning by using different types of question.' |

If the observer and person being observed have prepared well and the observer has made suitable notes, the post-session discussion should easily become constructive and straightforward. If you feel the feedback is just becoming descriptive, start thinking about the impact of what was observed. How do you know whether the participants learnt anything?

It is often good practice for the observer to invite the person they have observed to comment first on the training session or on the specific focus of the observation. The observer should then give honest feedback based on the *evidence* they have written down.

The feedback should focus on what happened in the training rather than on the trainer as a person. State, for example, that two people at the back were chatting off task rather than querying why the trainer failed to spot it. Or, 'I noticed that only a few people were participating in the discussion', rather than 'You are not very good at running plenary sessions.'

In this way, the discussion becomes solutions-focused, which is more productive than just listing problems. The conversation can then lead to next steps and, ideally, an action plan. Again, it is important that this is manageable, and that the focus is on one or a small number of items rather than everything. Part of the action plan might be a follow-up observation or observing someone else in action. The cycle of developmental observation is perpetual.

Even with many years of experience I still get nervous just before I am about to begin training – and even more so when I am being observed by colleagues!

I was recently involved in co-presenting some training to teachers who were keen to become trainers themselves. Many of them already had some training experience, but they were attending the two-day course to improve and enhance their trainer toolkits.

As part of the training, each teacher had to prepare and present a 15-minute showcase to their peers and the trainers (myself and my colleague). Throughout the training my colleague and I illustrated training techniques, discussed effective modes of delivery and all of the other essential ingredients. However, the final piece of help we offered was for one of us to present our very own 15-minute showcase to the group – me!

I put everything we had talked about into practice and delivered my 15-minute showcase. It went really well, and I was pleased overall. However, I was very conscious that my co-presenter, two other colleagues and 16 teachers were watching me. And then we invited the teachers to critique my showcase. Bizarrely I really liked this part! It was great to have other people's opinions and see how they had viewed certain decisions that I had very consciously made. I was able to offer my rationale for choosing to use coloured pieces of paper, or limited text on the slides, etc. Importantly, I also learnt what I could modify for next time.

After the event I took a few moments to think about the process of being observed. Although I was nervous I wasn't anxious or worried. Why? I think because I had prepared very well, I had practised the showcase before having to 'perform' it and I was confident in my abilities as a trainer. I also knew that we can always improve as trainers and as a result my training toolkit would be a little more enhanced!

# MENTORING AND COACHING

As schools, organisations and companies increasingly understand the value of investing in their people, more are offering opportunities for mentoring and coaching. The training world is no exception, especially as the role of the trainer can be quite isolated. Many books and articles have been written about mentoring and coaching but let's take a brief look at each in turn from the perspective of a trainer who wants to improve their practice.

The intention of both mentoring and coaching is to help people develop. They have much in common but are not the same thing.

According to Starr (2014), 'A mentor is someone who takes on the role of a trusted adviser, supporter, teacher and wise counsel to another person.' Mentoring typically involves an experienced professional working with a less experienced colleague and can last a long period of time.

> The mentor gives support . . . in a way that empowers the mentee. An effective mentor is able to stay flexible to the needs of the mentee in order to offer the appropriate types of assistance in a particular situation. (Starr, 2014).

The mentor does not dominate the relationship or impose their own priorities but rather responds to the needs of the person they are mentoring. Being a useful and successful mentor has more to do with personal qualities and inter-personal skills.

Coaching, according to Gallwey (1974), is 'unlocking a person's potential to maximize their own performance; helping them to learn rather than teaching them'. It is about developing a person's skills and knowledge so that their performance improves.

The goal of the coach is to build 'awareness, responsibility and self-belief' (Whitmore, 2009). It is not about telling another person what to do on the basis of your own experience, but to facilitate new ways of thinking and being, including how to remove 'internal obstacles' such as a lack of self-belief.

Coaching normally has a set duration and involves regular, structured meetings between the coach and coachee. The focus is on specific areas of development and how to achieve goals that the coachee (or the organisation for which they are working) determines. The coachee should do most of the talking, prompted by open, 'WH' questions (such as what, where, who, when, why and how) from the coach.

There is some overlap between the two, but Table 13.2 provides a general summary.

**Table 13.2**   Comparison of mentoring and coaching

| Mentoring | Coaching |
| --- | --- |
| Broad, developmental | Specific goals |
| Advising, supporting, challenging | Questioning, listening, facilitating |
| Longer-term, more informal | Shorter-term, more structured |
| Mentor is usually an expert in the topic | Coach need not be an expert in the topic |
| Mentor usually does most of the talking | Coachee usually does most of the talking |

You may already be able to see how both mentoring and coaching could work in the context of training. Perhaps mentoring is more suitable for new trainers and coaching for those who are more experienced – although it need not be as distinct as that. Someone who has trained for years may need mentoring on a new topic; someone who is just starting as a trainer may quickly identify specific areas for development through coaching.

Depending on your needs but regardless of your experience as a trainer, consider who could act as your mentor or coach. Think as well about how you could, in due course, mentor or coach other trainers.

If you read more about coaching, you will soon come across the GROW model, first written about by Whitmore in the 1990s. If you are giving feedback to another trainer about how they could improve, you might want to consider this model as a way of structuring the conversation.

Once you have thanked the trainer (if you have observed their session) and set the scene, lead them through the following four phases:

- **G**oal – ask them what they wanted to achieve in their training session;
- **R**eality – ask them to what extent they feel they were successful;
- **O**bjectives – ask them what were the challenges or what prevented success;
- **W**hat next – encourage them to commit to some steps to improve performance.

You will notice the use of open questions. Within each of the four phases you can ask other questions such as: 'What went well?', 'How could you have involved the participants more?', 'Where did you feel most comfortable in the room?', or "Why did that activity not go to plan?'

You can also simply invite the person you observed to describe aspects of what they did in the training session, such as: 'Tell me about the types of question you used', 'Describe the way you presented that activity', or 'Tell me how you got the group at the back involved.'

Alternatively, you could use scoring. Ask the person you observed to rate out of 10 how a particular activity went, how clear their instructions were, or how engaged their participants were before and after lunch. Ask them if the participants would give the same rating. Ask them what they would need to do to improve the score from a 4 to a 5 or an 8 to a 9.

This way, you are still giving feedback but the person you observed is taking a more active role. You are facilitating their thinking, helping them to break down the constituent parts of what it takes to be a trainer and take greater responsibility and ownership for how they might continually improve.

## TRAINING WITH OTHER TRAINERS

All three of us have observed, mentored and coached each other. We have also had the pleasure of planning training together and co-facilitating sessions. It is great fun to do if you get on well, mutually respect each other and have matching or complementary personalities as trainers. Training with other people offers a natural way to observe a colleague in action and to review the success of materials you have co-written.

We reminded you at the beginning of this chapter that the focus should be the *training* rather than the *trainer*. Of course, the skills of the trainer have a large impact on the success of the training. The point, though, is that for participants to learn something, the training must be well designed so it can be facilitated well.

If you are facilitating a session with another trainer, you must once again take time to plan. Make sure you have a common purpose and set of objectives, then work out together how you are going to meet these and who will lead each section. You should also take time after the training to reflect and evaluate, whether or not you will be co-facilitating the same session again. To make this more constructive and measured, use some of the observation and coaching techniques described above.

You may want to plan collaboratively with more than one other trainer to finalise how to run one specific session. If so, you may find it useful to try out the following three steps.

1.  **Plan** a training session together, focusing above all on what participants should be learning – think about everything we have discussed in this book, such as timings, the layout of the room, materials and the precise wording of questions.
2.  Choose one person to lead the session while the other trainers **observe**. Often it is a good idea to observe only a select number of participants or section of the room; observers should write down what they see, or video or photograph the session.
3.  After the session **reflect** together on how it went – as you jointly planned the session, you have equal responsibility for its success and whether learning took place. Ask each other open questions to elicit how successful the session was and what could, or should, be changed next time.

This is a highly collegiate approach to developing yourself as a trainer. You can learn from each other, play to your strengths and improve your weaknesses. It also makes the process of observation much less scary and makes what is being learnt central to the training.

## TOOLKIT CHECKLIST

When planning your training course, you can now ask yourself the following questions.

- Have I observed another trainer or asked another trainer to observe me?
- Have I identified two or three areas I would like to improve in my training?
- Have I asked someone to mentor or coach me?
- Have I planned training sessions with other trainers?

# 14

# SELF-DEVELOPMENT

## KEY WORDS IN THIS CHAPTER

- self-development
- importance
- investment
- standards

- recognition
- professional
- strengths
- development

### IN THIS CHAPTER YOU WILL:

- understand the importance of engaging in self-development as a trainer;
- recognise that effective CPD is an investment;
- reflect on your own personal and professional trainer standards and how to maintain these;
- complete your landing card.

As soon as you finish your session, you are likely to have several different thoughts:

- I am relieved it is over.
- I think it went OK.
- Did I cover everything I wanted to?
- What would I have done differently?
- Can I do it again?!

All of the above points are very natural reactions, but the last point is particularly interesting. You may have this reaction for several reasons: first, the training went really well and so you would like to repeat it; secondly, you missed out chunks of the session (purposefully or not) and so would like to do a re-run and see if you can include them; thirdly, you can already see how you could change or tweak the session to improve it further.

Whatever your reason, reflecting on the training session and how to improve it is a hallmark of an effective trainer. The drive to continually seek to improve practice will help you grow and flourish as a trainer. Everyone involved in education should have the opportunity throughout their career to build on their knowledge and skills and this includes trainers.

There is much diversity in professional learning and so recognising that we can all improve and knowing where to seek advice are the final pieces in our trainer toolkit for you.

# RECOGNISING THE C IN CPD

Continuing Professional Development (CPD) is an 'essential intellectual and emotional endeavour' (Guskey, 2005) but it is complex. This is because there is no 'one size fits all' model. What will work for one person will not necessarily work for another. Throughout this book, we have tried to show that the three of us have very different training styles and needs. While this makes us unique, it also creates challenges in the type of development needs we each have.

CPD can take many forms. It is a term used to represent a variety of different activities by different agents for different purposes. It can be explored as an individual or as a collaborative body. It can be informal or formal. But most importantly it should be based as much as possible on your needs as a trainer. However, the importance of the 'C' recognises the long-term aspect of development. Attending one course or reading one article is not going to sustain your development forever!

While all CPD is useful, some formats may contribute more towards *informing and influencing* as opposed to *embedding and transforming* you as a trainer. In other words, not all CPD may have a direct impact on your training. It might be that you gain some information that informs your knowledge further, but this may not directly affect how to set up the environment or decide which handouts to use.

# MAINTAINING YOUR OWN PERSONAL AND PROFESSIONAL TRAINING STANDARDS

Self-development requires a certain amount of self-reflection. The more you train the more you will know if you have delivered a good session. Of course, how we all define 'good' is very different and subjective. However, it is important to develop your own benchmark of what 'good' means to you. In doing this, you are creating your own set of personal training standards. These standards are not validated by anyone other than yourself, but it will give you immediate feedback about how your session went (before you read any evaluations or talk to any participants).

## TAKE A MOMENT

What would your own personal training standards be?
Can you write at least five?

However, you could seek out professional standards too. Around the world there are organisations that offer professional trainer standards. It is always worth exploring these and investigating their worth. Often these professional standards are accredited, ensuring that they have met set criteria and are quality controlled and assured.

Here are a few questions you might like to consider in deciding whether to invest, either in professional training standards or in some form of trainer accreditation:

- Is the organisation, set of standards or accreditation well known and well respected?
- How much does it cost financially (standards or accreditation)?
- How much time is required to complete the standard or accreditation?
- What do I get at the end of it (e.g. certificate, logo to use, email tag)?
- Are there any testimonials I can read from other trainers who have achieved this standard or accreditation?
- How long does the standard or accreditation last?
- What extrinsic value will I gain from having the standard or accreditation (e.g. further work, reputation, higher salary)?
- What intrinsic value will I gain from having the standard or accreditation (e.g. self-assurance, knowledge that I practise what I preach in terms of the importance of CPD)?

Of course, there are other ways in which you can maintain your own personal training standards other than completing a professional, accredited standard. Hopefully, by the time you are reading this section of the book you will have a better idea of the trainer characteristics you have. If not, remind yourself of your trainer characteristics that we talked about in **Chapter 3**. It is important to be able to recognise what you do really well and what is within your trainer traits to improve further. For example, we may all aspire to add a little comedy into our training but participants can tell if this is not part of your usual persona.

However, there are some critical features that all trainers can and should maintain to the highest level. Each chapter in this book has included a **Toolkit Checklist** which helps you to identify what you should be able to do after reading each chapter. Why not use these checklists to set a benchmark for your own trainer standards? You could employ a simple rating score of: achieved/more work needed, a RAG (red, amber, green) rating if you feel you need a little more flexibility or alternatively come up with your own way of benchmarking yourself. To help, we have gathered together all of the Toolkit Checklists and included them at the end of this book.

Once you have established your own standards for training you need to consider how to begin reflecting on and developing them through CPD.

There are also some CPD activities that are incidental or informal that may have value. You might seek professional development through, for example:

- reading an article, blog, book;
- engaging in informal conversations with other trainers;
- watching a YouTube clip or TED Talk;
- keeping up with the world of social media;
- joining professional associations (subject-specific or generic).

While these types of informal CPD activities do not directly offer the opportunity to watch a trainer move around the room or use a variety of activities, they do enhance your knowledge on another level. We can all be brilliant at motivating adults but if our content, subject or pedagogical knowledge is outdated or has gaps, the participants are not going to view the training favourably.

One final way to maintain your own trainer standards links straight back to that initial thought when completing a training session: *Can I do it again?* However, you may also think: *Will I do it again?* Perhaps at this stage you won't know if you are going to run the session again, but it is good practice to pause, reflect and edit.

So, try and take a few minutes to review your training session immediately. Ask yourself:

- What would you change?
- What worked really well?
- Did you have too much material?
- Did you have too little material?
- Did you provide the right resources?
- Would you choose to employ groups or pairs again for certain tasks?
- Did you think of anything mid-training that could be included next time?
- Did the timings work?
- Did the environment work or should you have adapted it?
- Did the training match the brief?
- Did participants react positively?
- Did participants gain what you hoped they would from the training session?

All three of us have got into the habit of evaluating training sessions immediately. We will spend a few minutes once participants have left and the room is tidied just sitting and going back through the materials. We then keep our notes in case we run the training session again. Invariably, you always change bits anyway, but having some notes that you have immediately jotted down does really help! Just as being a reflective teacher is good practice, so too is being a reflective trainer!

# TOP TEN TRAINER TIPS

We all agree that if we had been given a list of *top tips* when we began training, it would have really helped us. So, we have pooled our knowledge to produce the top ten tips for being an effective trainer in Table 14.1.

**Table 14.1**   Top ten trainer tips

1. Get to the training room with plenty of time. This allows you to set up, check equipment and then have a few minutes to relax before participants arrive.

2. Greet participants at the start of the session and always smile. The sooner you establish a relationship with them the better.

3. Within the first few minutes, give participants something to do. This could be a short task, the opportunity to talk or the chance to introduce themselves. It's important for them to be active very quickly.

4. Keep up the pace! Remember – training is different to teaching – so while you want to give enough time for participants to listen, learn and reflect, they are also responsible adults who can do more after the training event.

5. Use a lot of praise – encourage participants to feel they are doing well, and that they have really gained something from the session.

6. Keep an eye on the time, try to stick to the programme, but don't be afraid to adapt.

7. Over prepare! It is much better to have a variety of activities and a few extra – just in case!

8. Suggest follow-up tasks for the participants to do after the session has finished, including reflection.

9. It is handy to pack a few snacks and water in case you don't have time to take a break.

10. Leave enough time for your participants (and yourself) to evaluate the session.

## TOOLKIT CHECKLIST

When planning your training course, you can now ask yourself the following questions.

- Have I reflected on both formal and informal ways of developing myself as a trainer?
- Have I considered what my strengths already are and what I might need to work on next?
- Have I created my own top tips for being an effective trainer?

# FINAL REFLECTIONS

At the beginning of the book we introduced you to the idea of a *Boarding Pass*. We invited you to look at the grid on page 6 and rate yourself against each statement. Hopefully you have been able to try out some of the ideas and activities in the book, and so we are going to ask you to do the same activity again, but this time for your *Landing Card*.

Read the statements overleaf and circle the number that best describes your confidence level now. Again, be *honest* and remember there are no right or wrong answers. Rate yourself from 0 to 3 with the highest number meaning the highest confidence.

| | I feel confident that I . . . | | | |
|---|---|---|---|---|
| 1 | can plan a workshop to meet its stated objectives. | 0 | 1 | 2 | 3 |
| 2 | can prepare a range of suitable materials to engage and challenge my audience. | 0 | 1 | 2 | 3 |
| 3 | maximise the environment in which I am working to help my audience in their learning. | 0 | 1 | 2 | 3 |
| 4 | use a variety of presentation techniques to assist in the delivery of my topic. | 0 | 1 | 2 | 3 |
| 5 | understand how to encourage my audience to be active learners in the workshop. | 0 | 1 | 2 | 3 |
| 6 | can adapt the teaching and learning approaches I use for my audience according to their needs. | 0 | 1 | 2 | 3 |
| 7 | can ask, answer and encourage the use of questions. | 0 | 1 | 2 | 3 |
| 8 | know how to manage the behaviour and mindset of a diverse group of adults. | 0 | 1 | 2 | 3 |
| 9 | can help my audience to consider how to put into practice what they have learnt from the workshop. | 0 | 1 | 2 | 3 |
| 10 | have the tools to reflect on what went well and how I could improve my training even more. | 0 | 1 | 2 | 3 |

**Figure 14.1**   Landing Card

We have come to the end of our Trainer Toolkit.

We hope we have been able to support you in your thinking and development as a trainer.

Good luck!

Paul, Alison and Mark

# APPENDIX 1
# TOOLKIT CHECKLISTS

When planning your training course, you can now ask yourself the following questions.

## CHAPTER 1 – PROFESSIONAL DEVELOPMENT

1. Have I reflected on any recent training I have attended and considered what I can do with what I observed?
2. Have I considered the different styles/modes of delivery I have observed and what might be appropriate for the next training session I deliver?
3. Have I reminded myself about what professional development means to me and to others?

## CHAPTER 2 – KNOWING YOUR AUDIENCE

1. Have I thought about my audience?
2. Have I considered their individual needs?
3. Have I understood that my audience might have different ways of working?

## CHAPTER 3 – WORKING WITH ADULTS

1. Have I switched from thinking as a teacher to working as a trainer?
2. Have I reflected on the different theories of adult learning and considered how these might affect my next training session?
3. Have I put myself in the participants' shoes and viewed the training from their perspective?
4. Have I considered which training traits I might be employing?

5.  Have I reflected on the different reasons why the participants are attending the training?
6.  Have I thought how to motivate and empower the participants?

# CHAPTER 4 – DISSEMINATING LEARNING

1.  Have I considered how participants in my training will disseminate their learning?
2.  Have I thought about the different levels (students, teachers, departments, whole school) in a school at which my course may have impact?
3.  Have I designed a training course which will empower participants to cascade their learning?

# CHAPTER 5 – PLANNING

1.  Have I understood the *why* and the *what* of my training sessions?
2.  Have I thought about how to make the best use of my time?
3.  Have I structured my sessions effectively?
4.  Have I opened and closed my training sessions with impact?

# CHAPTER 6 – MATERIALS

1.  Have I made a list of the basic resources I will need in a training session?
2.  Have I learnt how to choose and design learning materials effectively?
3.  Have I understood the importance of intellectual property?

# CHAPTER 7 – ENVIRONMENT

1.  Have I found out about the environment ahead of the training session?
2.  Have I thought about the most appropriate arrangement of the furniture?
3.  Have I decided which props I would like to use?
4.  Have I viewed the training environment as an extension of my own character and personality?

# CHAPTER 8 – PRESENTATION

1.  Have I thought about the first impressions my participants will have of me?
2.  Have I considered how to set expectations for behaviour?
3.  Have I planned my sessions so that all participants feel included?
4.  Have I taken care with the style and difficulty of language I am using?
5.  Have I used presentation software purposefully?

# CHAPTERS 9–11 – TRAINING ACTIVITIES

1.  Have I chosen which activities I could use in my training sessions and at which stage?
2.  Have I understood the importance of knowing and using a variety of activities?
3.  Have I thought about the preparation and resources I will require?

# CHAPTER 12 – SELF-EVALUATION

1.  Have I thought about my own strategy for immediate evaluation of my training sessions?
2.  Have I understood the characteristics of different types of evaluation evidence and chosen appropriate evidence to evaluate my training at different levels?
3.  Have I understood how evaluation evidence is important to my own self-development?
4.  Have I made a plan for how to respond to negative feedback?

# CHAPTER 13 – OBSERVING AND BEING OBSERVED

1.  Have I observed another trainer or asked another trainer to observe me?
2.  Have I identified two or three areas I would like to improve in my training?
3.  Have I asked someone to mentor or coach me?
4.  Have I planned training sessions with other trainers?

# CHAPTER 14 – SELF-DEVELOPMENT

1.  Have I reflected on both formal and informal ways of developing myself as a trainer?
2.  Have I considered what my strengths already are and what I might need to work on next?
3.  Have I created my own top tips for being an effective trainer?

# APPENDIX 2
# TRAINER A–Z

| |
|---|
| A is for . . . **active** |
| *Your participants will switch off quickly unless you make them think and participate. Never just talk and expect them to listen.* |
| B is for . . . **breaks** |
| *Make sure participants know when breaks are going to happen; they may have planned phone calls, they may need to pray, etc. Don't forget that some of them will still be expected to respond to emails, even if they are attending training outside of school, especially if they are senior members of school staff.* |
| C is for . . . **collaboration** |
| *Include strategies that enable participants to collaborate during the training. This helps networking but also shares knowledge and experience between delegates.* |
| D is for . . . **discipline** |
| *Don't be afraid to ask for silence, for mobile phones to be switched off, or to encourage those participants who appear disengaged. The more explicit you are, the less chance of misunderstandings.* |
| E is for . . . **enthusiasm** |
| *Right from the start, make it clear that you are enthusiastic about what's to come. If you believe in what you are doing, so will they!* |
| F is for . . . **figuring things out** |
| *The more you require participants to figure things out, the more they will understand and achieve the objectives. It's not just about communicating ideas – your participants have to figure out the relevance of those ideas for their own context.* |
| G is for . . . **group work** |
| *Group and re-group participants for different activities. It helps them to learn from each other's knowledge and experience, particularly when re-grouped into mixed school groups, mixed subject groups, etc.* |
| H is for . . . **handouts** |
| *Think carefully about your handouts. Make sure they are clear, that any instructions are well explained and that they are useful. Participants like resources which they can 'take away' with them. Always plan for at least one 'take-away' resource.* |

I is for . . . **innovative**

*Try to ensure participants encounter new ideas; you want them to feel the training session has been worth it!*

J is for . . . **justify**

*Participants will ask you questions so be prepared to justify your ideas. Don't use a resource or activity which you don't understand yourself, and listen carefully to their questions.*

K is for . . . **knowledge**

*Successful trainers realise that their participants already have a lot of academic and professional knowledge. You should plan to engage with participants' prior knowledge and use activities which enable participants to build on that knowledge.*

L is for . . . **language**

*Make sure your language is clear and well thought out. If you have participants for whom English is a second or third language, help them by speaking slowly, and by including key messages on the PowerPoint slides (so they can read them slowly).*

M is for . . . **move**

*Move around the room during the training. You want to give participants the opportunity to ask you questions individually. Being 'out and about' among the participants also gives you a sense of whether a particular activity has been a success, who is engaging (and who is not), and whether participants are learning what you intended.*

N is for . . . **note**

*Note down anything which comes up which needs addressing with the whole group. Have a pen and notepad with you at the front of the room.*

O is for . . . **objectives**

*Always know what your objectives are, and share them with your participants. There is nothing worse than a training course which doesn't appear to have an aim.*

P is for . . . **pace**

*Think about what each individual will be doing during your course. Plan to maintain a strong pace, to keep participants engaged, and to make them feel their time is being used to best effect.*

Q is for . . . **questions**

*Ask open questions, to get your participants to think. WHY and HOW questions help to stimulate discussion and debate. If participants talk, they will think. Participants will also want to ask you questions so put a pack of sticky notes on the tables and ask participants to put any burning questions on a 'question wall', so you can deal with them at the right time.*

R is for . . . **reflect**

*Ask participants to reflect upon what they have learnt at the end of the session and ask them to reflect on their own classroom experience during the session. Helping them to realise what they've learnt, and how they can implement it is important for achieving impact.*

| |
|---|
| S is for . . . **show** |
| *If you want participants to do something, show them, tell them and write the instructions down.* |
| T is for . . . **trust** |
| *It is important for participants to trust you and your expertise. Introduce yourself at the start, making clear the credentials you have for running the training. Think about how the way you dress may gain their respect and trust.* |
| U is for . . . **understanding** |
| *Just as you would with school students, try to assess your participants' understanding of the objectives. Don't just settle for working out if they 'liked' the training: you need to know if they have learnt something.* |
| V is for . . . **variety** |
| *Plan your training to include a variety of strategies and activities. You don't want bored participants.* |
| W is for . . . **why** |
| *Make sure you explain to participants the purpose of activities, why they should complete them and what they should learn from them.* |
| X is for . . . **x-planations** |
| *Make sure your explanations are really clear. It's worth planning ahead and even putting the steps in the explanation onto the PowerPoint slide.* |
| Y is for . . . **you** |
| *You may feel nervous, you may feel apprehensive, particularly if it's your first training session. If you've prepared well, you will feel confident, and you can be happy that you're the expert, you're in charge and your training course has value to your participants. If you are confident, your participants will have confidence in you.* |
| Z is for . . . **zealous** |
| *Show the participants that you are zealous in your ambition for quality training and for participants' engagement and learning. They need to see professional slides, high-quality resources and you investing all your effort to secure a fantastic training experience. If you do that, they will do the same.* |

# REFERENCES

Chapman, A. (2015) Conscious competence learning model. *Business Balls*. Retrieved 23 February 2015 from http://www.businessballs.com/consciouscompetencelearningmodel.htm

Clay, B. and Weston, D. (2018) Five reasons why schools struggle. *Times Educational Supplement*. Retrieved 4 February 2019 from https://www.tes.com/news/5-reasons-why-schools-struggle-cpd

Gallwey, W.T. (1974) *The Inner Game of Tennis*. Toronto: Bantam Books.

Guskey, T. (2000) *Evaluating Professional Development*. Thousand Oaks, CA: Corwin Press.

Guskey, T. (2002) Professional development and teacher change. *Teachers and Teaching: Theory and Practice, 8*(3/4), 381–91.

Guskey, T. (2005) Foreword. In C. Day and J. Sachs, *International Handbook on the Continuing Professional Development of Teachers*. Maidenhead: Open University Press.

Knowles, M. (1984) *The Adult Learner: A Neglected Species* (3rd edn.). Houston, TX: Gulf Publishing.

Maslow, A.H. (1954) *Motivation and Personality*. New York: Harper.

Starr, J. (2014) *The Mentoring Manual: Your Step by Step Guide to Becoming a Better Mentor*. Harlow: Pearson Education.

Whitmore, J. (2009) *Coaching for Performance*. London: Nicholas Brealey.

# INDEX